Foreword

Lisa Brenninkmeyer

From the time we are little girls, we long for true friendship. We want to be seen, known, and valued no matter what. Knowing a friend has your back can give you the confidence to press on or to get out of a situation that has grown unhealthy. Friends make us laugh when we take ourselves too seriously and are there to brush off the dust when we've been down on the mat. They show up at the right time and commiserate with us over our disappointments, but also know when to encourage us to rise again out of the ashes. We weren't meant to journey alone, and friends can be one of God's greatest gifts to us.

Can you remember a time in your life when friendship seemed to come easier than it does now? When I think back to early elementary school, it just seemed like things unfolded naturally. My friendship with one of my best friends, Megan, had everything to do with where we both happened to live. We lived on the same block so it was easy to spend time together because we didn't need a parent to arrange a playdate or drive us anywhere. She was interested in playing "pretend" which turned into a love of the theater, and that mutual interest carried us through high school. It was the sheer number of hours logged that formed our friendship, that and the fact that she never stabbed me in the back and always stood up for me. I never worried about what she was saying about me when I wasn't around.

But things have gotten more complicated the older I've become. In my adult years, I have experienced my fair share of toxic friendships. And the thing that has caused me pause in recent years is the fact that I have fallen into the same patterns with female relationships time and time again. There was something I was missing—key indicators that this was not a good place for me to be investing my time—but I wouldn't pick up on it. And even if I did have a gut feeling that a friend wasn't good for me, I wasn't sure how to get out of the relationship.

This is why Mallory Smyth's Bible study, *Reclaiming Friendship*, has meant so much to me personally. She has unpacked what to look for in a friend, what the purpose of friendship is, and how to get out of unhealthy friendships. Her wisdom and grasp of Scripture make her a wonderful teacher and guide. She's had some excellent life experience as a FOCUS missionary on college campuses, which gives her additional insight into what it takes for women to relate to one another and truly connect.

There are points in our lives when we are wise to take stock of the state of our friendships. Are we investing our time in the right places? Are our motives pure, or are we looking at friendship from a selfish perspective? Have we fallen into comfortable patterns in terms of who we hang out with, but they are not bringing out the best in us? Are we at a crossroads where we realize that we don't have good friends, and the loneliness is starting to take a toll?

Proverbs 13:20 tells us that "he who walks with the wise grows wise but a companion of fools suffers harm." We are influenced by our friends, whether we like it or not.

Even Jesus gave careful thought to the choosing of his friends. He spent all night in prayer before choosing his twelve disciples, asking God to help him to discern whom he should surround himself with. He then chose three of the twelve (Peter, James and John) to be the closest of all.

What is it that attracts you to a woman? Is it her style? Her vibrant personality? Her graciousness? Her kindness? Her obedience to God? Are the qualities you are drawn to superficial ones, or ones that really matter in the long run? When we notice that someone is living the Christian life in a way that we admire, that's a good reason to consider going a little deeper with her.

It can be a costly mistake to choose someone who has a very different spiritual or moral foundation than you for your *best* friend. When the chips are down and you are in a crisis, you need a friend who can speak the truth in love and guide you to the right path. Too often, our friends just say what makes us feel good when they could have been used as instruments in molding us into women of wisdom and maturity.

One of the purposes of best friends is to help one another recognize blind spots. Proverbs 27:9 says, "The pleasantness of one's friend springs from his earnest counsel." And then Proverbs 15:31–32 teaches, "He who listens to a life-giving rebuke will be at home among the wise. He who ignores discipline despises himself, but whoever heeds correction gains understanding."

When we find a truly wonderful friend who is willing to speak truth in love and meets certain needs in our hearts, we need to check that we keep things healthy. True friendship is different from being codependent or needy. It was when reading the book

Friendships of Women by Dee Brestin that I first heard the term "relational idolatry." Relational idolatry takes place when we allow a person to take a place of importance in our life that was meant only for God. We can become so dependent on a friend that we cease to be dependent on God. That is not a healthy balance.

Author Larry Crabb talked about how in a fallen world we wrongly associate certain things as breeding life or death to our souls. The dynamics of a relationship can feel like a "source of life." Then, when that person withdraws slightly, it feels like death. Depending on a friend as your source of life ultimately leads to bondage. God is the true source of life. And when a relationship has Him in the middle of it, there is freedom.

In a healthy friendship, we point our girlfriends to Christ, not to us. Our friendships should be like a braid, three pieces woven together—the two friends and God. Dee Brestin writes of 3 warning signs that things are out of balance:

- You experience frequent jealousy, possessiveness, and a desire for exclusivism, viewing other people as a threat to the relationship.

- You prefer to spend time alone with this friend and become frustrated when this does not happen.

- You become irrationally angry or depressed when this friend withdraws slightly.[1]

Let's check ourselves to make sure that we don't allow anyone the place in our hearts that has been reserved for God alone. He is the only one who will never let us down. If we place a friend in that position, we are sure to be disappointed.

One thing we know about God, He is always willing to help us experience a fresh start. You do not need to content yourself with the status quo. It is within your power to make new friends, walk away from unhealthy ones, and chart a new path towards meaningful connection, accountability, and joy.

It is my prayer that as you go through *Reclaiming Friendship*, your relationships with women will become more life-giving and your relationship with God will deepen further still. I pray that you would connect with sisters in Christ who share your goal to become a woman of purpose, supporting and encouraging you on that journey. I pray that each one of us would follow God's pattern for friendship and experience the deep satisfaction that comes from His love being made complete in us (1 John 2:5).

---

1 Dee Brestin, *Friendships of Women* (Victor Books, 2008), 86.

of women who have flourishing, God-centered friendships.

...self to the world through friendship. I also believe that God wants us to

walking with purpose

Dear friend,

What has been your experience with friendship? Some of us have great, life-long, loyal friendships. Others of us have been wounded by the women we trusted the most. For some of us the word friendship brings up fond memories, fun, and laughter. For others it brings up drama and conflict that we would rather forget. Most of us have experiences that are in between. No matter your experience, I wrote this study with you in mind and have been praying for you every step of the way.

Sister, you were created in the image of God. This is a big deal. You reflect a unique part of Him to the world. You are a gift to your friends and your friends are a gift to you. God invites us to live our lives in holy, joy-filled friendships with other women. Too often, we forgo this invitation and allow the culture to dictate the terms of our friendships. Because of this, our friendships never quite reach the potential for which God designed them. But I am convinced that the Lord has a plan for our friendships that goes beyond what we can ask or imagine.

In this study, we are going to dive into God's purpose for friendship, the wounds that we experience, the ways we can heal, and then ultimately how we can become the type of women who have flourishing, God-centered friendships. I believe that God wants to reveal himself to the world through friendship. I also believe that God wants us to grow deeper into friendship with Him.

Do you know that His love for you goes beyond mere obligation from Creator to creature? He loves you with the perfect love of friendship. He delights in you and finds joy in who you are. He thinks that you are funny and creative, and He wants you to reclaim the gift of friendship so that you can experience more of His joy with others here on earth in a way that will bring you closer to Him in heaven. He wants to redeem you, He wants to redeem your friendships, and I am honored to dive into His word with you.

In His heart,

Mallory Smyth, Walking with Purpose

Reclaiming Friendship

God's Plan for Deep Connection

RECLAIMING FRIENDSHIP

Mallory Smyth

walking with purpose

∽ SO MUCH MORE THAN A BIBLE STUDY ∽

www.walkingwithpurpose.com

Authored by Mallory Smyth

The recommended Bible translations for use in Walking with Purpose studies are: The New American Bible, which is the translation used in the United States for the readings at Mass; The Revised Standard Version, Catholic Edition; and The Jerusalem Bible.

Any internet addresses (websites, blogs, etc.) in this book are offered as a resource and may change in the future. Please refer to www.walkingwithpurpose.com as the central location for corresponding materials and references.

21 22 23 24 25 / 12 11 10 9 8 7 6 5 4 3 2 1

ISBN: 978-1-943173-34-1

Reclaiming Friendship: God's Plan for Deep Connection

Printed in the United States of America

TABLE OF CONTENTS

INTRODUCTION

LESSONS

APPENDICES

ANSWER KEY

PRAYER PAGES

Welcome to Walking with Purpose

You have many choices when it comes to how you spend your time—thank you for choosing Walking with Purpose. Studying God's Word with an open and receptive heart will bring spiritual growth and enrichment to all aspects of your life. Every moment you invest will be well worth it.

Each of us comes to this material with a unique vantage point. You are welcome as you are. No previous experience is necessary. Some of you will encounter questions that introduce you to concepts that are new. For others, much of the content will be a review. God meets each one of us where we are. He is always faithful, taking us to a deeper, better spiritual place, no matter where we begin.

The Structure of *Reclaiming Friendship*

Reclaiming Friendship is a six-session Bible study that integrates Scripture with the teachings of the Roman Catholic Church to answer the core question, "What is God's vision for friendship, and how can I experience it?" As we strive together to reclaim God's plan for friendship and connection, we will see that understanding God's character is a central piece of understanding our relationships.

For those who are participating in Walking with Purpose in a group context, four weeks of this study will be spent in small groups discussing one of the lessons from the *Reclaiming Friendship* Bible study guide. Twice during the study, participants will gather for a Connect Coffee, which consists of social time, a video presentation of the related Bible study talk, and small group discussion. Anyone doing this study on her own will find it simplest to watch the videos online, using the URLs provided with the talk outlines. There are also four shorter videos to accompany Lessons 2-5. In a group setting, you may choose to watch these together. If time doesn't allow, we encourage everyone to watch these videos at home as they provide excellent supplemental material.

Study Guide Format and Reference Materials

The *Reclaiming Friendship* Bible study guide is divided into three sections:

The first section comprises six lessons. Most lessons are divided into five "days" to help you form a habit of reading and reflecting on God's Word. If you are a woman who has only bits and pieces of time throughout your day to accomplish tasks, you will find this breakdown of the lessons especially helpful. Each lesson includes an introduction; a conclusion; a resolution section, in which you set a goal for yourself based on a theme of the lesson; and portions of the *Catechism of the Catholic Church (CCC)* that are referenced in the lesson.

For the two Connect Coffee talks in the series, accompanying outlines are offered as guides for taking notes. Questions are included to guide your group's discussion following the video.

The second section, the appendices, contains supplemental materials referred to during the study, as well as an article about Saint Thérèse of Lisieux, the patron saint of Walking with Purpose.

The third section contains the answer key. You will benefit so much more from the Bible study if you work through the questions on your own, searching your heart. This is your very personal journey of faith. The answer key is meant to supplement discussion or provide some guidance when needed.

At the end of the book are pages intended for weekly prayer intentions.

Bible Recommendations

What were your thoughts the first time you picked up a Bible? Perhaps you got one as a gift for confirmation or graduation. Maybe it was a copy you found lying around at home. It could be that the first time you held a Bible was in a classroom setting. Which of these two statements better reflect how you felt in that moment: "I just can't wait to dive into these pages because I know it'll be life changing" or "This looks boring and inaccessible. I'm sticking it on my shelf." For most of us, it was the latter.

One of our goals at Walking with Purpose is to teach women how to use the Bible as a practical, accessible tool. There are some obstacles in the way of that happening. One problem is how we approach the Bible. If we open it up in Genesis and start reading through from start to finish, we will likely have trouble understanding what is going on (and we'll probably quit once we get into Leviticus). One of the reasons this method can be confusing is because Scripture is not a book; it's a library. This library is filled with many genres: poetry, letters, historical narrative, and apocalyptic writings. When we don't know what genre we are reading, we can quickly become frustrated. For example, reading Genesis as a science book instead of as inspired poetry will cause us to see faith and science at odds. Far too many people write off Christianity because they feel it can't possibly be true after seeing discrepancies between things proven by science and the way the same things are described in the Bible. This is a consequence of not recognizing the Bible as a *library* of Truth, utilizing many genres of literature to lead us to the heart of God, understand His story, and see our place in the epic tale of redemption. Catholics don't read everything in the Bible literally. We read some things literally, but not everything.

Another obstacle to using the Bible as a practical, accessible tool for spiritual growth is not knowing where to begin. This is exactly why Walking with Purpose has created Bible studies and programs like BLAZE. Being guided through Scripture, being led to the passages that are most applicable to life in the 21st century, helps the Bible to come alive.

You may also want to consider Bible tabs as a resource. It takes about thirty minutes to put Bible tabs into a Bible, but it makes it so much easier to find your way around Scripture with these markers. You can find Bible tabs at Catholic bookstores or online. Be sure to get the Catholic version as Protestant versions of the Bible are missing seven books of the Bible. (At the time of the Reformation, the books of Sirach, Tobit, Wisdom, Judith, 1 and 2 Maccabees and Baruch as well as portions of Daniel and Esther were removed in order to embrace a canon of Scripture that reflected Protestant theological beliefs. Books were never *added* to the Catholic Bible—they have always been there.)

We recommend using either the NABRE (New American Bible Revised Edition) or the RSVCE (Revised Standard Version, Catholic Edition) translations.

Walking with Purpose™ Website

Please visit our website at www.walkingwithpurpose.com to find additional free content, supplemental materials that complement our Bible studies, as well as a link to our online store for additional Bible studies, DVDs, books and more!

WWP Scripture Printables of our exclusively designed verse cards that compliment all Bible studies. They are available in various sizes and formats, perfect for lock screens, and a format that allows you to email them to a friend.

WWP Playlists of Founder Lisa Brenninkmeyer's favorite music accompany each Bible study.

WWP Videos of all Connect Coffee Talks.

WWP Blog

For a weekly dose of inspiration and encouragement from our bloggers. Subscribe for updates.

WWP Leadership Development Program

Do you long to see more women touched by the love of Christ, but aren't sure how you can help? We are here to help you learn the art of creating community. It's easier than you think! God doesn't call the equipped; He equips the called. If you love God and love women, then you have what it takes to make a difference in the lives of people around you. Through our training, you'll be empowered to step out of your comfort zone and experience the rush of serving God with passion and purpose. You are not alone, and you can become a great leader. We offer the encouragement and the tools you need to reach out to a world that desperately needs to experience the love of God

Join Us on Social Media

facebook.com/walkingwithpurpose

twitter.com/walkingwpurpose

instagram.com/walkingwithpurpose_official

youtube.com/walkingwithpurpose_official

pinterest.com/walkingwpurpose

Lessons

Walking with Purpose is a community of women growing in faith – together! This is where women are gathering. Join us!

www.walkingwithpurpose.com

Lesson 1: Connect Coffee Talk

TRUE FRIENDSHIP AND ITS FRUITS

Accompanying talk can be viewed by DVD or digital download purchase or access online at walkingwithpurpose.com/videos.

I. **A Look at True Friendship**

A. Friendship is a relationship that is not connected through blood or romance but out of a simple desire to _____, _____, and _____.

B. "Friendship is the only love that is absolutely deliberate."[2] –Tim Keller

C. "There is nothing on this earth more to be prized than true friendship."[3] –St. Thomas Aquinas

D. "When you gain a friend, gain him through testing, and do not trust him hastily. For there is a friend who is such at his own convenience but will not stand by you in your day of trouble. And there is a friend who changes into an enemy and will disclose a quarrel to your disgrace. And there is a friend who is a table companion but will not stand by you in your day of trouble. In your prosperity he will make himself your equal and be bold with your servants; but if you are brought low, he will turn against you, and will hide himself from your presence. Keep yourself far from your enemies and be on guard toward your friends." (Sirach 6:7–13)

E. "A faithful friend is a sturdy shelter: he that has found one has found a treasure. There is nothing so precious as a faithful friend, and no scales can measure his excellence. A faithful friend is an elixir of life, and those who fear the Lord will find him. Whoever fears the Lord directs his friendship aright, for as he is, so is his neighbor also." (Sirach 6:14–17)

II. The Fruits of Intentional Friendship

Loyalty – Ruth and Naomi

Ruth 1:16 – *where you go I will go your God is my God...*

Comfort in Sorrow – Jesus, Martha, Mary, and Lazarus

John 11:31–36

Thru our friendships God offers US his comfort

"It doesn't always have to look like tears. It can look like playdates - simply showing up and watching your friend's kids while she naps or cries or takes a bath. It can look like planning an extra meal a week and delivering it whether she asked for it or not… Just being a buffer between her and her grief, a physical reminder that she is not physically alone with her sorrow. Laying down our lives for our friends can translate into a hundred daily inconveniences that simply remind her without using actual words, 'You are not alone.'"[4] –Lisa-Jo Baker

Support – Mary and Elizabeth

Luke 1:39–43

"When the Holy Spirit in one woman recognizes and responds to the Holy Spirit in another woman, safe places become sacred places."[5] –Sophie Hudson

---

4   Lisa-Jo Baker, *Never Unfriended* (Tennessee: B&H Publishing Group, 2017), 118.
5   Sophie Hudson, *Giddy Up, Eunice* (Tennessee: B&H Publishing Group, 2016), 118.

Foretaste of Eternal Friendship with God – David and Johnathan

1 Samuel 18:1

Eventually King *↳ King Saul Son*

2 Corinthians 4:17

Questions for Discussion

1. Write below about the friendship in your life that has brought you the most joy. What about this relationship brought you delight?

    Kelly
    ✓ Nancy

2. The Book of Proverbs repeatedly claims that people suffer from the lack of friends or from poorly chosen friends. Do you agree or disagree? Why?

3. Do you experience loyalty, comfort, and support in your friendships? Are there ever elements of drama and dysfunction? What changes would you have to make for your relationships to resemble the friendship with God that we will experience in heaven?

→ Loyalty – sticks closer than a family than not obligation

Looking for more material? We've got you covered! Walking with Purpose meets women where they are in their spiritual journey. From our Opening Your Heart 22-lesson foundational Bible study to more advanced studies, we have something to help each and every woman grow closer to Christ. Find out more:

www.walkingwithpurpose.com

NOTES

Faithful friends are a life-saving medicine; those who fear God will find them. SIRACH 6:16

Full-Color Free Printables available at walkingwithpurpose.com/free-printables

Lesson 2

WHAT IS FRIENDSHIP?

Introduction

When I was eighteen, I traveled to Franciscan University to watch my brother Jared and his fiancé Katie graduate from college. Franciscan University is known for its vibrant Catholicism and is attended mostly by young men and women who are serious about their faith. After the graduation ceremony, I sat with my parents and watched Jared and Katie visit with their friends. Unable to hear their conversations, I simply observed them. I was struck by the way Katie and her friends interacted. Knowing almost nothing about them personally, it was clear to me that they honored one another with joyful attention. I sensed from them a peace and a joy that I wanted.

Years later, in the courtyard of my sorority house, I remembered Katie and her friends. After spending three years away from my faith in college, I had decided to give Christianity another try. I didn't even know where to start. I looked at the women scattered outside and compared the nature of the friendships around me to what I had seen years ago at my brother's graduation.

I had to ask myself, "Do I have friends like Katie did? Do I share something with my friends that goes beyond a few activities and a slew of acquaintances?" I had friends. I knew that with the exception of a few women, most of my relationships were based on my social scene. Women who were "fun" surrounded me, but I only felt safe enough to fully reveal my heart to a few of them. While we had good intentions, we often affirmed each other in our vices instead of challenging each other to become better. While we certainly had love for one another, our love was often endangered by gossip, comparison, and insecurity. We were never too far from the drama that can instantly turn friends into frenemies. I sat in the courtyard wondering if what we had experienced was *true* friendship.

Can you relate?

Have you ever spent years in a friendship only to learn that you had been betrayed? Have you ever thought you had a best friend only to find out that she didn't feel the same? Have you allowed your own insecurities to extinguish the warm feeling you once felt toward someone? Most of us can recall the hours spent replaying a conversation in our head as we try to figure out what we said and what she said. No matter our stage of life, middle school drama plays out on the field of friendship. Most of us have been mortally wounded at one time or another.

It wasn't meant to be this way.

Katie and her friends shared something, or Someone, different than most friendships share. The secret of their friendships was that the foundation of each relationship rested on God. God is the creator of friendship. He meant for friendships to be one of the primary sources of joy in life, places where we can learn to love and be loved.

Could it be that friendship is complicated because modern culture values self and comfort above all else? These are very different from what God values and sets us up for constant conflict. If we are willing to rewire our friendships according to how God designed them to work, then we will find deep love and true joy in our friendships.

Let's find out what God wanted for us when He created the beautiful gift of friendship.

Day One
FROM THE BEGINNING

In order to understand God's plan for friendship, we have to lay some groundwork. Today, we go back to the very beginning to understand why relationships are so important and why we were created in the first place. To do this, we are going to dive into the first chapters of Genesis.

Before we begin reading, we must understand how the Catholic Church interprets the Bible. As Catholics, we believe that the Bible is inspired by the Holy Spirit and is completely true. The Church teaches that there are different genres and styles of writing throughout the books of the Bible. To understand Scripture, we must pay attention to the type of text we're reading. The first two chapters of Genesis are written in poetic language; they tell us the truth about creation in the form of poetry. We do not take these first two chapters of Genesis literally. Instead, we look for the beautiful truth conveyed by this part of the Bible.

1. Read Genesis 1:1–3.

    Who created the heavens and the earth in Genesis 1:1? Who was hovering over the waters in Genesis 1:2?

2. A. In the beginning, God the Father created the world, and the Spirit of God was hovering over the waters. Who else was there according to John 1:1?

    B. What do we learn about the identity of the Word of God from John 1:14?

Many people think of God creating the world and Jesus coming along thousands of years later. But what we learn from the book of Genesis and the Gospel of John is that the Father, the Son, and the Holy Spirit were all together at the beginning of creation.

According to the *Catechism of the Catholic Church* (CCC) 234, "The mystery of the Most Holy Trinity is the central mystery of Christian faith and life." Bishop Robert Barron described the Trinity as an interplay of relationship, "of love, being loved, and shared love."[6] God the Father is the lover, God the Son is the beloved, and their perfect exchange of love is personified in God the Holy Spirit. If the relationship of the Holy Trinity is perfect love and perfect intimacy, and if we could add nothing to its perfection, it might cause you to wonder why God created us in the first place.

3. A. Did God need something from us? Read Acts 17:24-25.

    B. If God needs nothing and is not served by humanity, why did He create us at all? Read CCC 1.

    C. According to CCC 221, for what are we destined?

---

6 Bishop Robert Barron, "Bishop Barron on the Meaning of the Trinity," YouTube video, 9:44, June 22, 2017, https://www.youtube.com/watch?v=5l-Lv9tGQwI.

Some of the deepest questions in the recesses of our hearts are "Why am I here?" and "What is my purpose?" These questions have plagued even the most brilliant thinkers for all of human history, but the answer has always been there. CCC 1 tells us that "God, infinitely perfect and blessed in himself, in a plan of sheer goodness, created us to share in his own blessed life."

4. A. According to CCC 27, where will we find truth and happiness?

    B. What does it say that we must do to live fully according to the truth?

5. If we need to accept God's love and entrust ourselves to Him to live according to the truth, we need to learn how to do that. This process is explained in Appendix 2, *Conversion of Heart*. Read it and reflect on what you've read. Is this something you have experienced personally?

Quiet your heart and enjoy His presence. . . Seek Him first and the rest will be added.

You were not created for restlessness but for peace. You were not created for loneliness but for intimacy. You were not created out of need, but out of desire—God's desire to bless the world with your unique soul. In Him you will find the truth and happiness for which you are searching.

Saint Augustine said that we will be restless until we let ourselves rest in Him. It should be so simple. Yet, what the Lord requires of us, ourselves, our hearts, seems like too much to ask. We spend our lives on the hamster wheel, searching for love and purpose in all the wrong places. If our life does not flow from our relationship with God, everything else becomes unbalanced. We find ourselves exhausted, hidden, and lonely. Overwhelmed by this emptiness, we put pressure on other relationships to fill us and validate us in a way that only God can.

He offered us more from the beginning and His invitation still stands. In Psalm 139:1–4 King David wrote about just how deeply the Lord knows us. "You have searched me, Lord, and you know me. You know when I sit and when I rise; you perceive my thoughts from afar. You discern my going out and my lying down; you are familiar with all my ways. Before a word is on my tongue you, Lord, know it completely." Sit with these words in prayer. Ask God to reveal to you the ways that you resist sharing in His life. Surrender those ways to Him.

Day Two
WE BELONG TO EACH OTHER

On Day One, we established that God made us to be in a relationship with Him. First and foremost, we were made to know God and be known by God. Today, we will learn about another relationship God created us to have.

1. Read Genesis 2:7–9, 15–23.

    A. God created Adam out of the dust and breathed life into him. What did God say in Genesis 2:18?

The Hebrew word for "alone" is "levaddov" which can also mean "separation" or "apart."[7] When God said that it is not good for man to be alone, He declared that the human race is distinct from all creatures. We were created with a need to live with other human beings.

    B. What did God do in Genesis 2:21–23 to provide a suitable helper for Adam? How did Adam respond?

2. Pope Saint John Paul II said, "Man becomes the image of God not so much in a moment of solitude but in a moment of communion."[8] God's intention with our creation was always relationship—and not just with Him.

    A. Read CCC 1878. What is inseparable from the love of God?

    B. According to CCC 1879, what does the human person need? How will man reach his full potential?

God meant for our relationships with others to give us a foretaste of what we will experience in total intimacy with Him. He meant for us to belong to each other joyfully and completely. In the garden of Eden, that was Adam and Eve's experience. But in our own lives, this is often far from our reality. Right after Adam proclaimed that he had at last found a suitable helper in Eve, the couple fell from grace. At the prompting of the serpent, the couple ate the fruit which God had forbidden. Recognizing their sin, they hid from God.

3. Read Genesis 3:12–14. How does Adam respond when God asks why He ate the fruit from the tree in the garden? How does Eve respond to God's question?

The moment that Adam and Eve sinned in the garden, the intended nature of the human relationship was shattered as shame and blame entered the picture. What was supposed to be our greatest source of earthly joy and belonging became our greatest source of earthly pain. Betrayal, manipulation and deceit moved in where there was once only love, self-gift and honesty. Is belonging to each other even worth it? It seems like it would be so much easier to keep people at an arm's length while we embrace our pets. Why not lean on self-sufficiency rather than risk authentic, vulnerable relationships? Refusing relationships can feel good at first, even empowering, but eventually we find ourselves alone and unknown. Instead of belonging to each other, we carry unseen burdens that were never meant to be hidden and never meant to be carried alone.

4. Reflect on the relationships in your life. Have you been bruised by past relationships? Do you find it easier to hide your true self from others? Does hiding part of yourself from others keep you from experiencing the joy that God meant for you to experience in relationships with others?

5. A. If it was through Adam and Eve's sin that the nature of our relationships was broken, where is our hope? See John 3:16–18.

    B. How did He model this type of love for us? See John 13:1–12.

    C. What new commandment did Jesus give to His disciples in John 13:34–35?

Quiet your heart and enjoy His presence. . . How good it is when we dwell together in unity.

"If we have no peace, it's because we have forgotten that we belong to each other."[9] *—Saint Teresa of Calcutta*

Everything in our world tends to lead us away from true connection with each other. From the lonely relationships we have with our screens, to our desires to do it "our way," to our fear of putting ourselves out there only to be hurt again, relationships feel like too much risk. But what about the joy that we experience when we find a true, authentic, and lasting connection?

Vulnerability researcher Dr. Brené Brown defines connection as "the energy that exists between people when they feel seen, heard, and valued; when they can give and receive without judgment; and when they derive sustenance and strength from the relationship."[10]

This is the kind of connection that we were meant to have in relationships. This is the kind of connection that Jesus redeemed for us in His life, death, and resurrection. So how do we live it? Saint Paul tells us in Ephesians 4:2–3, "Be completely humble and gentle; be patient, bearing with one another in love. Make every effort to keep the unity of the Spirit through the bond of peace." Are we humble, gentle, and patient with those around us? Or do we enter into our relationships from a place of selfishness and need for validation? Let us first examine our own hearts when we look at the health of our relationships.

We know that on this side of heaven, we can do everything from a place of genuine love and our relationships may still suffer. Know dear sister, that even in those moments, you are not alone. Jesus sees, understands, and is present. Ask Him to lead you to people in your life with whom you can find genuine connection and then lean in with love.

---

9   Saint Teresa of Calcutta, "Mother Teresa Reflects on Working Toward Peace," *The Architects of Peace*, Santa Clara University, 07/12/20, https://www.scu.edu/mcae/architects-of-peace/Teresa/essay.html.

10 Brene Brown, *The Gifts of Imperfection* (Minnesota: Hazelden Publishing, 2010), 19.

Day Three
DEFINING FRIENDSHIP

We have established that we were made for relationships with God and others. Now let's take our focus to friendship. Friendship is at the heart of all good relationships, but it is a loaded term. Similar to the words "love" and "beauty," "friendship" means vastly different things to different people. Some have experienced friendships characterized by love, joy, and self-sacrifice. Others associate friendship mainly with drama, manipulation, and betrayal. As women, our experiences in friendship are varied. For us to be able to explore God's purpose for friendship, we have to be working from the same definition. So let's define our terms.

1. Read Sirach 6:14–16.

    A. List below the attributes used to describe a faithful friend.

    B. Who finds and enjoys these friendships?

2. A true and trustworthy friend is priceless.

    A. What kind of instructions are we given in Sirach 6:5–6 regarding the ways we should relate to people?

These verses describe gracious and friendly interactions with other people. We should strive to interact with every person this way, even if she is not our close friend. One might describe the relationships with these kinds of people as "acquaintanceships," not friendships. There is something slightly negative about the word "acquaintance," isn't there? So we try not to use it. Since we have weird associations with the word "acquaintance," we call people "friends" when we really don't know them all that well. In the German language, the word for acquaintances doesn't bear any negative connotation. A woman is a *bekante* until she becomes trustworthy. At that point, she becomes a *freundin*. Being considered a *bekante* isn't an insult; it's an accurate description of the level of intimacy. We lack the equivalent description in English, which sometimes causes our expectations of people who aren't close, trustworthy friends to be unrealistic.

> B. In your experience, are all friends faithful? How many close confidants are we advised to have in the second part of verse 6?

> C. Why should we be slow to trust new friends according to Sirach 6:7–8?

These verses in the book of Sirach reveal to us what we already know from experience. Not all friendships are equal. There are different levels of goodwill and loyalty shared between friends. Some friends will stick with us through thick and thin, others will disappear at the first sign of trouble, and others will fall somewhere in between. We should absolutely expect there to be variations in our friendships.

Dr. John Cuddeback, professor and author, defines friendship as, "A mutually recognized relationship of affection that occurs between human persons, who have the maturity to bear some kind of goodwill for one another."[11] For example, we can have goodwill toward a baby, but the baby does not have the maturity to recognize, respond, and share the same type of goodwill. While the relationship may be a beautiful one, it is not a friendship. For a friendship to exist, both people need to be at similar maturity levels, and recognize and share well wishes with each other.

Aristotle, the famous Greek philosopher, wrote that there are three types of friendship. What the English language lacks (and what the German language offers) Aristotle provides with these descriptions. These distinctions are helpful tools. It's important to be able to define what kind of friendship you are talking about.

Useful friendships: Useful friendships are transactional in nature. Each person in the relationship gets something out of it. Business relationships are an example of useful friendships. Once the transaction ceases to continue, so does the relationship.

Pleasurable friendships: Pleasurable friendships are based on having a good time together. Women who party together are an example of pleasurable friendships.

---

11 John Cuddeback, *True Friendship: Where Virtue Becomes Happiness* (Denver: Epic Publishing, 2010), 27.

Other types of pleasurable friendships may be friendships that spring up from two women attending the same workout class, or their kids playing on the same sports team. This type of friendship runs a bit deeper than a transactional friendship, but the heart of the relationship is based on enjoyment of the other's company. If the framework for enjoying each other's company ceases to exist, such as a workout class or sports season coming to an end, so does the relationship.

Virtuous friendships: Virtuous friendships are not based on a transactional exchange or simply having a good time together. What sets virtuous friendships apart from useful and pleasurable friendships is that the women choose to invest in each other. Useful and pleasurable friendships fall into our laps through the activities in our calendar, but when we decide to invest our lives in each other, a useful or pleasurable friendship can transform into something deeper. The heart of virtuous friendship is the desire for the other person's good. Each person is loved for her own sake. In these friendships, we find the unwavering loyalty and support that we think of when we think of true friendships. In these friendships, each person challenges the other to become better.

3. While all types of friendships can be good, the deepest of these friendships is virtuous friendship. Friends love each other for who they are, and each person wants the best for each other. Jesus took virtuous friendships to another level. What does Jesus say is the greatest way we can love in friendships? See John 15:13.

4. Jesus laid down His life for us when He went to the cross so that we could live in friendship with the Father. He laid down His life for us, whom He called friends, and challenged us to do the same. Saint Paul reflects this type of friendship in his first letter to the Thessalonians. Saint Paul had relationships with Christians in cities across the ancient world, but there was something different about his relationship with the Thessalonians. Read 1 Thessalonians 2:8. What was Saint Paul delighted to share with them? What type of friendship did he have with them?

To lead each other to the ultimate and highest good, true friendship must center on Christ. To become our true selves is to become like Jesus, and to find true joy is to submit our lives to God in every relationship. When friendships are viewed in this context, they take on a new depth. This doesn't mean that every conversation becomes a prayer session. This means that everything in the friendship flows from a desire for each woman to become who God made her to be.

5. Write down the names of some of your closest friends. How would you characterize each friendship? Do you have more useful, pleasurable, or virtuous friendships?

6. Do you have friendships that could be virtuous but aren't? What do you think is keeping your friendship from going deeper? What is one thing that you can work on to bring that friendship to the next level?

Quiet your heart and enjoy His presence. . . He calls you a friend.

Not all of Jesus' relationships were deep, intimate friendships, but they were all good. From His walking with people on the road, to sitting and laughing with friends at the Wedding at Cana, to sharing the deep mysteries of His Father's Kingdom with his closest apostles, Jesus experienced every form of friendship.

Take solace in the fact that you do not have the capacity to make every single friendship deep, soul sharing, and virtuous. Some of your friendships are meant to be deep and virtuous. Others will be lighter—useful or pleasurable—but in all of them Jesus asks you to follow His example and enter with the gaze of love for the other, exactly the way He looks at you.

Dear Lord,

Thank You for the women that You have placed in my life and for all of the ways that You have shown me Your goodness through my friendships. I know that my friendships should help to lead me to You, but honestly it doesn't always feel that simple. My friendships can feel so messy. Gossip, comparison, and drama seep in. Lord, I ask for Your forgiveness when I have failed to love my friends well. I ask for Your healing in the places of my heart that my friendships have created a wound. I invite You into my friendships. Please make Your home at the center of these relationships. Enable me to love other women well so that in the end, our friendship reflects Your goodness to the world. Amen

Day Four
TRUE FRIENDS ENABLE US TO LIVE A HAPPY LIFE

In virtuous friendships, each person loves the other for who they are, not what they can do for each other or get out of the relationship. They desire the very best for each other and together strive to become the best versions of themselves. This type of friendship is ideal but it's not easy. Most of our friendships rarely progress past the experience of a good time. Pleasurable friendships, as nice as they are, can't make us truly happy. God calls us to more, and He gave us a way to cultivate virtuous friendships. Today we will explore how God enables us to love more deeply in our friendships and how that type of love affects our lives.

Read John 15:4–13.

1. In John 15, Jesus sat with His closest friends at the last supper. He knew that this was the last time that He would sit with the men who had been with Him for the past three years. Jesus used this moment to tell his friends—who certainly would have been in the "virtuous friendship" category—what was most important to Him. Rewrite John 15:4–8 in your own words.

2. Jesus tells His apostles in the first part of John 15:9, "As the Father has loved me, so have I loved you."

   A. What does Jesus say in the second part of verse 9?

   B. How are we able to abide in Jesus? See John 15:10.

   C. What will we have if we abide in Jesus according to John 15:11?

   D. In the very next breath (15:12), Jesus gives His apostles a commandment. What is that commandment?

Jesus followed up His command to "Love each other as I have loved you" and said, "No one has greater love than this, to lay down one's life for one's friends." Shortly after He said this, He went to the cross for all of mankind. Jesus called all of us to sacrificial, self-giving love—the kind of love that makes us willing to sacrifice our time, our preferences, our very lives, for the good of another.

He knows that we don't have it in us to love this way on our own. That is why He told us that we can do nothing apart from Him, absolutely nothing (John 15:5). We can try to love with sacrificial love apart from God, but we will always fall short.

On the other hand, He told us that if we live in His love, we will bear much fruit. When we abide in God, we allow Him to define how we see ourselves and how we see others. His love becomes our love, and it flows out of us and into our relationships. This is the sure way, the only way, for us to experience the type of relationships that God desires for us. If we lean on Him, we'll experience the transformation that comes to our friendships when we cooperate with Him.

3. God tells us in Scripture that friendship is a good thing, bringing us more joy than the material pleasures in which we often delight. There is something about spending time with virtuous friends that makes us feel safe, refreshed, happy, uplifted, and supported.

    A. Read Ecclesiastes 4:9–12. What do friends do in time of need?

    B. How do friends help each other to grow according to Proverbs 27:17?

    C. What two things did the apostles do in Acts 2:46 that gave them glad and generous hearts?

4. We have all had friendships that have gone wrong. Eventually we will dive into the behaviors that cause our friendships to fail, but for today, think of the friendships in your life that have brought you the most joy. What is it about those specific friendships that has been the most satisfying?

Quiet your heart and enjoy His presence… Two are better than one.

When God said that it is not good that man should be alone, He knew we needed each other to be happy. He knew working together, generously helping each other, brings a type of joy to our hearts that working alone cannot. He knew we would suffer in our broken world, so he gave us friends who would stretch out their hands to help us during hard times. He knew that in true, virtuous friendship we could challenge each other to become better versions of ourselves, closer to the women God created us to be. He also knew that we would find joy and rest in fellowship, enjoying one another's company, and glorifying God in our midst. In friendship, we celebrate the unique way that God placed His very own image into someone else and our friends celebrate how God has placed Himself in us.

Dear Lord,

Thank You for the ways that You have blessed me through my friends and used me to bless others. In my closest friendships, I have the honor of witnessing Your unique glory in others. Give me Your eyes so that I can see my friends the way that You do. Give me Your mind so that I can value these friendships the way that You want me to. Thank You for bringing me joy in these relationships. Help me to become the kind of virtuous friend that loves others the way that You have loved me. Amen.

Day Five
FRIENDSHIP TEACHES US TO LOVE

As we explored yesterday, God wants our lives to be marked by joy and happiness. While we certainly are meant to experience joy in our friendships, God's purpose for friendship goes deeper. Today, we will examine how God uses friendship as a tool to help us to become people who love like He loves.

1. In Ephesians 4:1–2, Saint Paul urges us to live lives that are worthy of the call we have received. How does Saint Paul describe this type of life in verse 2?

2. Becoming people who truly know how to love can be confusing because there are many modern definitions of love. To "love," according to Saint Thomas Aquinas, is to "will the good of the other."[12] To will the good means to want the best for someone. We understand that the best is not what's immediately pleasurable

---

12 Saint Thomas Aquinas, *Summa Theologica*, (Stanford U.P., 1950), question 26, article 4.

or easy. Anyone who loves must be willing to encourage others to choose the best, even when it involves difficult interactions and conversations. This can look different in different situations.

A. Saint Paul defines love in Romans 12:9–13. How does he instruct us to love?

B. How does Saint Paul encourage us to love one another above ourselves in Philippians 2:1–3?

We can say that we love the "people" of the world. We can pray for them and we should. But a group of "people," in a general sense, doesn't require our time, energy, and sacrifice. It's "persons" who need that. "Persons" are the flesh and blood individuals who are directly in our lives. They need favors, limit our freedom, hurt our pride, and require our forgiveness. Pope Saint John Paul II said, "Love consists of a commitment which limits one's freedom—it is a giving of the self, and to give oneself means just that: to limit one's freedom on behalf of another."[13]

This is why friendship is so essential in learning to love. Friends require something of us—some sacrifice, small or large. Friends take up time that we had planned for something else. Friends call us out when we are falling short of who our friends know we are meant to be. They are in the mess, figuring it out with us. It is in these relationships, the imperfect, up close, and personal ones, where we will be transformed. If we want to be selfless, friendship is a great place to start. It provides countless opportunities to choose to follow Saint Paul's challenge to honor others above ourselves. This is hard. At this juncture, at the meeting of our wants and the needs of our personal relationships, we learn how to truly love by laying down our preferences and desires for the sake of honoring others above ourselves.

3. Can you think of a time when a friend loved you or you loved a friend in this sacrificial way? Share your experience here.

---

13 Pope Saint John Paul II. *Love and Responsibility*, (San Francisco: Ignatius Press, 1993), 135.

4. What does it look like when we allow ourselves to be inconvenienced by the needs of a friend? Read Mark 2:1–12 and recount the story in your own words. Explain what Jesus was doing, what the men did to get their paralyzed friend in front of Him, and His response.

The people who brought their friend to Jesus were probably not planning on unlatching a roof and causing a scene in front of a major crowd that day. They saw that the needs of their friend were more important than their pride or their plans. The man on the stretcher was probably not looking to inconvenience his friends, either. Allowing them to bring him to Jesus was an act of love in itself.

5. For some of us it is very difficult to accept acts of love and generosity from others. It is easier to give than receive because receiving love from others makes us feel vulnerable—even worse, needy or clingy. Do you struggle more with giving love or receiving love? Why?

Quiet your heart and enjoy His presence… His heart is moved by the love of friends.

In the television series about Jesus' life, The Chosen, *there is a beautiful scene in which Jesus heals the paralytic. At the beginning of the episode, a young woman happens to come across Jesus as He heals a leper. Seeing His power, her mind immediately turns to her friend who is paralyzed from the waist down. She gathers her group together and they carry their friend on a stretcher only to find Jesus unreachable through the crowds.*

As they try to push through the crowds, Peter and Mary Magdalene approach them. Mary tries to help them get to Jesus but sees no way through. She apologizes for the size of the crowd and says, "I don't want to interrupt the Teacher by causing a scene." Desperate, the young woman with the paralytic turns to Mary and asks, "Wouldn't you want your friends to make a scene?"

Mary realizes in that moment that she was once as crippled as the paralytic and is only restored because of Jesus. With her help, the paralytic and his friends get onto the roof, and again, the woman advocates for her friend as she boldly calls down to Jesus, "Jesus of Nazareth. I saw what you did to the leper on the road this morning. My friend has been paralyzed since childhood. He has no hope but You, please do for him what You did for the leper. If You are a willing Rabbi, I know you can do this."[14]

In a dramatic scene, the group carrying the crippled man unhinges part of the roof and lowers the paralytic down to Jesus who looks up at them, deeply moved by their audacious faith. Jesus looks at the woman and says, "Your faith is beautiful." In response to the powerful showing of love, Jesus heals the paralyzed man. God's heart is moved by the love of friends.

Do you see your friendships as an opportunity to perfect your love? Would you go further for your friends, honoring them above yourself? Do you recognize that Jesus really is your only hope and do all that you can to lay your friendships at His feet? Would you let your friends carry you to Him if you were unable to move? Bring these questions to the Lord today.

Conclusion

In 2019, actors Shia Lebouf and Zack Gottsagen made a heartwarming film called *Peanut Butter Falcon*. The movie is about a young man, Zak, played by Gottsagen, with Down Syndrome who escapes an assisted living facility to chase his dream of becoming a professional wrestler. Completely alone with nowhere to go, Zak hides on a boat that belongs to Tyler, played by Lebouf, a thief and fisherman with a hardened heart. Tyler discovers Zak on his boat and tries to leave him behind. He eventually changes his mind and lets Zak travel with him after he sees Zak being bullied by a young boy.

At first their friendship is purely transactional: Zak needs protection and Tyler doesn't want the guilt of abandoning a man with Down Syndrome. As the plot progresses, however, so does their friendship. The men get to know each other and start to enjoy each other's company. Tyler eventually agrees to take Zak to the home of his favorite wrestler.

Their friendship deepens from adventure to adventure. Tyler teaches Zak how to swim and shoot a gun. He even convinces Zak's favorite wrestler, long retired, to put on his wrestling suit and teach Zak to wrestle. All the while, Zak causes Tyler to let down his guard and discover parts of himself that he had blocked off. By the end of the movie, they have developed a deep love for each other. They both have built a virtuous friendship.

---

14 *The Chosen*, "Indescribable Compassion," 6, directed by Dallas Jenkins, 2020, Vidangelapp.

While the movie is endearing, what makes it so special is that the two actors developed a deep friendship in real life. In an interview with HeyUGuys, Labeouf told the audience just how much of an effect Gottsagen had on him. When the interviewers asked Lebeouf how the experience of filming the movie changed him, this is how he replied.

> It wasn't so much the experience; it was just being around Zack. He softened me, and if you were around him enough, he'd soften you too. You know, I was raised on Nirvana and the Simpsons. I have a really cynical gene in me that sort of overwhelms the naive cutesy part of me. You get around Zack long enough and you start feeling the effects...the biggest take away from the movie is that I walked away with a dude I love.[15]

God knows the power of friendship because He created it. Our earthly friendships are so powerful because they are a foretaste of the joy we will experience when we get to heaven and enter total union with God. While we are on earth, our friendships remind us that we are not alone. Others are here to walk with us. Friendship has the power to smooth out our sharp edges. It teaches us how to live in joy and harmony with others. It challenges us to move outside of ourselves, to love more deeply and enjoy life more fully. If God is the center of your friendships, His goodness and joy will be revealed to you and to those around you.

Want to learn more about this week's topic? Don't miss Lesson 2's short video from Mallory at walkingwithpurpose.com/videos.

My Resolution

"My Resolution" is your opportunity to write down one specific, personal application from this lesson. We can take in a lot of information from the Bible, but if we don't translate our knowledge into action, we have missed the point. In James 1:22, we're told that we shouldn't just hear the word of God, we are to "do what it says." Resolutions inspire us to put our knowledge into action. What makes a good resolution? It should be **personal** (use the pronouns I, me, my, mine), it should be **possible** (don't choose something so far-fetched that you'll just become discouraged), it should be **measurable** (a specific goal to achieve within a specific time period) and it should be **action-oriented** (not just a spiritual thought.)

Examples:

1. I will take account of my conversations with friends this week and ask myself, "Did this conversation help either of us to reach for the best version of ourselves?" If not, I will write down what we could do better in the future.

2. I will take time to reflect on who has been a true friend to me in my life. I will pray for that person every day this week and send them a note thanking them for how their friendship has impacted me.

3. I will spend an hour in the adoration chapel this week thanking the Lord for His friendship and asking Him to reveal how I can make my friendships more virtuous.

My Resolution:

Catechism Clips of the Catholic Church

CCC 1 God, infinitely perfect and blessed in himself, in a plan of sheer goodness, freely created man to make him share in his own blessed life. For this reason, at every time and in every place, God draws close to man. He calls man to seek him, to know him, to love him with all his strength. He calls together all men, scattered and divided by sin, into the unity of his family, the Church. To accomplish this, when the fullness of time had come, God sent his Son as Redeemer and Savior. In his Son and through him, he invites men to become, in the Holy Spirit, his adopted children and thus heirs of his blessed life.

CCC 27 The desire for God is written in the human heart, because man is created by God and for God; and God never ceases to draw man to himself. Only in God will he find the truth and happiness he never stops searching for: "The dignity of man rests above all on the fact that he is called to communion with God. This invitation to converse with God is addressed to man as soon as he comes into being. For if man exists it is because God has created him through love, and through love continues to hold him in existence. He cannot live fully according to truth unless he freely acknowledges that love and entrusts himself to his creator".

CCC 221 God's very being is love. By sending his only Son and the Spirit of Love in the fullness of time, God has revealed his innermost secret: God himself is an eternal exchange of love, Father, Son and Holy Spirit, and he has destined us to share in that exchange.

CCC 1878 All men are called to the same end: God himself. There is a certain resemblance between the unity of the divine persons and the fraternity that men are to establish among themselves in truth and love. Love of neighbor is inseparable from love for God.

CCC 1879 The human person needs to live in society. Society is not for him an extraneous addition but a requirement of his nature. Through the exchange with others, mutual service and dialogue with his brethren, man develops his potential; he thus responds to his vocation.

NOTES

NOTES

NOTES

NOTES

Lesson 3

THE BARRIERS TO FRIENDSHIP

Introduction

Prior to writing this study, I asked fifty women to share with me their personal experiences with friendship. The first question I asked was, "What is your biggest heartache when it comes to friendship?" These were some of the responses I received:

"A couple of friends wrote me off literally without any explanation. These were people who I thought were lifelong friends, but when whatever happened happened (I don't know!), they bailed instead of seeing our friendship as worthy of a hard conversation or confrontation."

"Friends get jealous and as a result they find it hard to share in my joy. They mourn with me well, but comparison has been a thief. I find I don't bring my whole self to many relationships—I don't talk about what is going on unless it's negative."

"I've felt like someone is my closest friend, but then realized that they don't quite feel the same."

"My biggest heartache is that I am not always the friend I want to be, and that has cost me some valuable friendships in the past. I am a natural introvert, so I need women who will hang on through my tendency to withdraw a little bit and who will give me grace when I don't connect as often as I should or in ways that I should."

Other common themes were gossip, broken trust, and comparison. It is this kind of behavior that typically characterizes female friendships in popular media. Ladies, we have earned it. We can be brutal to each other. In a world where it seems mean girls rule, all of us have hurt and have been hurt.

Saint Paul warned us about the consequences of this type of selfish behavior in Galatians 5:13–15 when he said, "For you were called to freedom, brethren; only do not use your freedom as an opportunity for the flesh, but through love be servants of one another. For the whole law is fulfilled in one word, 'You shall love your neighbor as yourself.' But if you bite and devour one another, take heed that you are not consumed by one another."

In this passage, Saint Paul speaks about the kind of spiteful behavior that can be found in so many female friendships. In Christ, we have been set free, but all too often, we ignore that we have been given freedom for a purpose: to love others as we love ourselves. Instead, we use our freedom as an opportunity to satisfy our flesh. We seek selfish gain and validation in our friendships. We easily fall into the bad behaviors that bring about the drama that wounds us.

In the last lesson we learned that God meant for our friendships to be a source of joy, a reflection of Him in which each person is loved for their own sake. Most of us have experiences that are a far cry from that vision. We carry with us baggage and insecurities from our past that affect our current friendships. In this lesson, we will explore barriers to friendship. We are going to unpack some of the pain points of friendship and how we can begin to move forward into friendships that are healthy and life-giving.

Day One
TIME

When we think about our deepest, richest, longest lasting relationships, time is often a key element. There is something special about sitting with a dear friend and recalling memories from what seems like a lifetime ago. Time is a great forger of friendship, but it also can be a great barrier. Many of us have more on our schedules than we know how to handle. The time we need to create deep friendships with others is hard to come by. We need to know how God is asking us to manage our time, especially when it comes to our friendships.

1. Read the following verses and write below how life is described.

    Psalm 103:15–16

    Psalm 90:5–6

Psalm 144:3–5

Psalm 39:5

2. Because we exist inside of time, a life spanning years seems long. Yet over and over again, Scripture speaks of the brevity of human life. What seems like forever to us is merely the blink of an eye to God. Read Psalm 90:12. What do we gain if we learn to number our days?

Psalm 90 is the oldest of the Psalms and was written by Moses. At the end of his life, he reflected on what he wanted to pass on to the next generation. In Psalm 90:11, Moses asked God to make us aware of our mortality so that we would be compelled to live with intention—to make time for what matters most.

Lydia Sohn, writer and Methodist minister, sat down with the members of her congregation who are in their nineties to get to know them. Her first question to them was, "What are your regrets?" Most of them answered that they wished that they had given more time and attention to their relationships.[16] In the twilight of their lives, they did not focus on their accomplishments, career success, or wealth. Their memories of joy and sorrow were all about their relationships. This reminder of what really matters should compel us to use our time intentionally.

3. Jesus only had three years of public ministry and was aware that His time was limited. In Matthew 17, Jesus reveals His glory in the Transfiguration. He could have revealed His glory to all of His apostles, but He chose not to. Who does Jesus reveal himself to according to Matthew 17:1–3?

4. Jesus served and performed miracles for large crowds, but He was only intimate friends with a few. Who are the women with whom you want to cultivate deep

---

16 Lydia Sohn, "I interviewed a bunch of 90-somethings about what they regret most and their answers surprised me," Business Insider, 9/28/2018, https://www.businessinsider.com/biggest-elderly-life-regrets-2018-9.

and lasting friendships? How can you give the right amount of time to those relationships so that they can flourish?

5. Living with intention means understanding the state of life we are in and how it directs the way we spend our time. What does Ecclesiastes 3:1 tell us to recognize so that we can properly order our time?

6. The amount of time we have to invest in friendship directly corresponds to our season of life and set of circumstances. No matter our age or life circumstance, there are challenges to finding time for friendship.

    A. Reflect on your season of life. What opportunities and challenges do you experience when you try to give time to the relationships in your life?

    B. List the three most important friendships in your life. How can you be intentional and creative about making time for those three? For example, you could set up regular time in your calendar to connect with a friend who lives far away. One morning a week could be reserved for spontaneously reaching out to friends nearby. You could even invite a friend into your busy-ness, to run errands or help you with a project.

Quiet your heart and enjoy His presence... Let Him direct your priorities.

Ephesians 5:14–17 says, "Therefore it is said, 'Awake, O sleeper, and arise from the dead, and Christ shall give you light.' Look carefully then how you walk, not as unwise men but as wise, making the most of the time, because the days are evil. Therefore do not be foolish, but understand what the will of the Lord is."

There are two modern myths that we believe when it comes to our schedules. The first myth is that we can live a balanced life in which we are giving everyone, and everything, the attention we feel they desire. The second myth is that we can get everything done if we just commit to the proper scheduling system.

Neither of these are true.

We can't achieve the "balance" that is championed by Instagram feeds. It is impossible to accomplish everything. Anyone who insists on trying will eventually end up crumbling under the pressure. Life is too short for us to chase such fantasies. Instead, the Lord calls us to give our time to what is most important in His eyes. Proverbs 16:9 says, "A man's mind plans his way, but the Lord directs his steps." He wants us to be organized and intentional with our plans, but He wants the last word. He wants to direct our steps so every part of our lives, including our friendships, reveal His glory. Is this perspective influencing your life? Are you giving others grace to follow the Lord's plan for their day? As women, we tend to take it personally when our friends are hard to pin down. Most likely, they want to spend time with us but are struggling with the same time constraints that we are. Instead of harboring stories in our head which leads to hurt feelings, we can offer them the grace and patience that we so often need ourselves.

Dear Lord,

You have created time as a gift to me. One day, I will behold Your face for all eternity. Until then, teach me to use my time wisely. Give me the wisdom I need to live my days well. Give me direction. With whom should I spend the most time? How should I be serving others the way that You did? I ask forgiveness for the times that I foolishly squandered the days You have given, and I forgive those who did not have time for me. Give me Your eyes so that I may see the moments that You give me as You see them. Amen.

Day Two
BROKEN TRUST

Broken trust in our friendships can be crushing. The pain of betrayal runs deep, and lasting effects can bleed into other relationships. Hurt doesn't have to have the last word. God has given us the power to heal from the betrayals we have suffered in the past, to ask forgiveness for our own failures, and to prevent from happening in the future.

1. Read Psalm 55:12–14. Throughout this Psalm, David cries out to God in sadness bordering on despair. David reveals in verses 12–14 that he has been betrayed. How does David describe his betrayer in verses 13 and 14? What had they done together?

Scholars believe that David wrote this Psalm about his close friend and trusted advisor, Ahithophel. David thought of Ahithophel as a friend, but Ahithophel conspired against David to help David's son Absalom take the throne.[17] When David found out what Ahithophel had done, he was devastated. His heart was in anguish, he was overcome by trouble, and was distraught by the noise of the enemy (Psalm 55:2–3).

2. Reflect on a time that you experienced broken trust in a relationship. What caused that trust to be broken? How did you feel at the time that trust was lost, and how was the situation resolved?

Whether you were betrayed, a lie was revealed, or you were manipulated for another's gain, the moment you discover broken trust can be crushing. The feelings that David expressed are feelings that many of us know well. We can't ignore these feelings. Moving on isn't simple. We have to acknowledge the wrong and our feelings if we want to get to the other side of pain and find forgiveness.

3. In Matthew 5:43–45, Jesus explains that it is common to love our friends and hate our enemies. What does He command us to do in verse 44? Why does He command us to do this in verse 45?

G.K Chesterton remarked, "The Bible tells us to love our neighbors, and also to love our enemies; probably because generally they are the same people."[18] People are complicated. Make no mistake, this is a hard teaching. In the midst of confusion and heartbreak, the last thing that we want to do is raise our eyes to heaven and pray for the one who hurt us. Most of us would rather overanalyze the situation and come up with all of the reasons why we are the spotless victims. Turning to God first is easier said than done,

---

17 Matthew Henry, *Commentary on Psalm 55*, Blueletter Bible, 9/20/2020, https://www.blueletterbible.org/Comm/mhc/Psa/Psa_055.cfm?a=533012.

18 G.K. Chesterton, *The Illustrated London News*. Jan 13, 1906.

but Jesus didn't tell us this to help us feel pious or to gloss over real pain. Following God's will has practical benefits.

4. Read Psalm 55:16–19. To whom does David call, complain, and moan to when he has been betrayed?

Proverbs 10:12 says, "Hatred stirs up strife, but love covers all offenses." When we sit too long in the pain of heartache, we end up creating more strife in our hearts and in our relationships. When we turn to God with our issues and pray for those who have hurt us, we turn away from hate and toward love. When we bring our broken relationships to the Lord, He reveals the truth to us. He may show us that the situation isn't as black and white as it seems. He may reveal to us that we played a part in the trust that was broken. He may show us that we need forgiveness, too. He may reveal the way to mend the relationship or tell us that this is the time to walk away. We should not ignore the very real work we have to do to move past the pain, but God sets our movement in the right direction when we go to Him first.

Quiet your heart and enjoy His presence… Let us learn from Him.

In Jesus' final hour, He was betrayed by two of His closest friends. Judas handed Jesus over to the authorities for thirty pieces of silver, and Peter, afraid for his life, denied ever knowing Him. Jesus knows the pain of betrayal, and He knows how it happens.

It is possible that Judas' betrayal was a result of small issues that he had with Jesus (see John 12:4). Peter's fear of rejection was stronger than his loyalty to Jesus. Terrified of the consequences of association with Jesus, he chose self-protection over courage.

When we allow the little things to build up over time instead of bringing them into the light with love, we run the risk of a blow up. The right opportunity comes along, and our frustrations lead us to make choices that we wouldn't have made otherwise. When we are constantly worried about what we will gain from our friendships, we run the risk of betraying another for the sake of ourselves.

Where are you in your friendships? Has this happened to you? If so, who heard about your pain? If you haven't brought it to God, it's ok to do it now. He sits with you, wanting you to know that He understands.

Dear Lord,

Thank You for Your radical forgiveness. Thank You for offering forgiveness in an instant even when Your closest friends broke Your trust. Give me Your heart, Lord, so that I can see others the way that You see them. Show me how You see me so that I will not be overwhelmed by the noise of the enemy, and instead would rest in the truth of Your sweet gaze. Forgive me for the times that I have broken trust with my friends knowingly or unknowingly. I offer forgiveness to those who have broken my trust. You are my hope and my stronghold, and I trust You to guide me as I navigate my friendships. Amen

Day Three
GHOSTING

Ghosting occurs when a close friend with whom you spend a significant amount of time suddenly disappears from your life. They cut off contact and communication. When this happens, the woman who is ghosted is almost always left with an intense feeling of confusion and insecurity. With no explanation and no closure, she must figure it out alone. What went wrong? The woman who ghosts, however, has usually been building up to it for a while. Let's take a deeper look, explore why ghosting happens, and learn how God wants us to handle these situations.

1. In Luke 19, Jesus enters Jerusalem. He asked His disciples to bring Him a colt so that He could ride into town.

    A. Read Luke 19:35–38. What did the disciples do to show Jesus honor in verses 35 and 36?

    B. Who sang praise to Jesus in verse 37, and what did they say in verse 38?

Jesus entered Jerusalem to songs of praise from a whole crowd of followers but that joyful time didn't last long. Six days later, Jesus celebrated the Passover meal, or the Last Supper, with the twelve disciples. After they finished their meal, Jesus took Peter, James, and John to pray. Soon after, He was arrested. In these moments, the disciples' loyalty to Jesus was tested.

2. Read Mark 14:43–50. Describe how the scene unfolded and write exactly what we learn in verse 50.

Only a week earlier, Jesus' disciples were glued to His side, entering Jerusalem in glory. They had three years of intimate history, traveling from town to town with Jesus as He shared life with them and revealed to them the secrets of the kingdom of God. Yet, in one moment, the moment when Jesus would have needed them most, they were gone. Every single person that Jesus called friend, except John, suddenly disappeared from Him.

It's easy to pass judgement on the disciples. They should have been loyal to the Son of God. They should have stuck with Jesus, but they didn't. When tensions got too high, their weakness trumped their friendship. They did the only thing they could think to do—they ran. Haven't we all been there at one point or another? According to a study published in the *Journal of Social and Personal Relationships*, when 1,300 participants were asked if they had ever ghosted someone or had been ghosted, 25% reported that they had ghosted someone, and 20% reported that they had been ghosted.[19] What we see in the behavior of Jesus' closest friends and followers is a common human behavior.

3. During the Last Supper, Peter had an exchange with Jesus. In John 13:36–38, Peter asks Jesus where He is going. How does Jesus respond in verse 36? How does the conversation end in verses 37 and 38?

Jesus knew that His disciples did not have the faith or understanding to walk with Him through His darkest trial. It's not that the disciples didn't want to be there for Jesus. They did. Peter even said that he would go so far as to lay his life down for Him. Their spirit was willing, but their flesh was weak. When Jesus was arrested to be taken to His death, fear set in and their weakness was revealed. The situation was simply too big for them to handle. They lacked the proper understanding and the proper maturity to stick close with Jesus through the worst trial of His life.

---

19 Gili Freedman, Darcey N. Powell, Benjamin Le, Kipling D. Williams, "Ghosting and destiny: Implicit theories of relationships predict beliefs about ghosting," *Journal of Social and Personal Relationships* 01/12/2018, https://journals.sagepub.com/doi/abs/10.1177/0265407517748791.

Friendships end for a whole host of reasons. Sometimes life is overwhelming, and a woman disappears from her friendships because she is going through something that she just can't share. As a result, she cuts everyone out of her life. She won't return calls or answer text messages because she is overwhelmed and doesn't believe that those in her life will care or understand. Instead of reaching out, she retreats into herself, cutting off those who love her the most.

Other times, a friend suddenly stops a relationship because the other person in the relationship is experiencing something difficult. It feels like this event consumes the energy that was once devoted to the friendship. Lacking the maturity for communication, neither friend says anything about the new dynamic. The ghosting might feel abrupt, but it's been a long time coming—the friend can no longer take it and ends the friendship by running away.

Other friendships that come to halt may not fit into either of those scenarios. It is possible that someone in the friendship is going through a normal life transition that redefines the roles that others play in her life. Things like getting married, welcoming children, getting a new job, or caring for an elderly parent are expected parts of life, but they may take up significant time. Due to the new rhythm of life, friends are less available for different seasons. If these changes aren't talked about, it may be perceived that a friend fell off the face of the earth without explanation. Maybe she was simply dealing with busy life transitions. Although not intentional, this is still hurtful to the one who feels left behind.

4. Have you ever disappeared from a friend or had a friend disappear on you? Reflect on the experience below. How did you feel when it happened? Do you know what caused the break? Do you have regrets about how it played out?

5. The sudden disappearance of a friendship isn't as sudden as it seems. There is typically a buildup of unhealthy behaviors that leads to the end of a friendship. We run and hide. We're left with confusion and hurt. This is not what God wants for our friendships. According to Ephesians 4:15, how should we address these behaviors in our friends and what will this help us do?

Speaking the truth in love requires Christ-like maturity. One of the ways we grow to be more like Christ is to strive to see others through His eyes. Jesus could always see who a person wanted to be at their core and who a person could be at their very best. When we see our friends through God's eyes, suddenly it becomes worth it to be honest about what's going on in the relationship. The risk of speaking the truth is worth it. The exchange, however awkward, becomes about what is best for each person.

What has happened in the past has already happened. If we have been hurt or have hurt someone by fleeing from a friendship, the Lord wants us to either forgive or to ask for forgiveness. In our current friendships, God calls us to be honest. We must open the door to loving, honest communication with our friends. It is ok to acknowledge the realities of a friendship as long as it is done in kindness. When we have the courage to do this, just as Ephesians 4:15 says, we will grow up into Christ. We will reach the maturity and understanding that is necessary for the development of healthy, virtuous friendships.

6. Consider your current friendships.

    A. Are there small tensions building that could easily be diffused by speaking the truth in love? What keeps you from being honest? How would that honesty affect your relationship with your friend?

    B. Sometimes we don't realize that there is something in our own behavior that is helping to contribute to the slow buildup of tension in friendship. Take a moment to honestly reflect on the interactions and conversations you have with your friends. Are you trustworthy? Do you keep confidential secrets to yourself? Do you give as much as you take from your friendship? In what ways can you change behavior to grow into Christ-like maturity in your friendships?

Quiet your heart and enjoy His presence. . . He will never abandon you.

"Can a woman forget her nursing child, that she should have no compassion on the son of her womb? Even these may forget, yet I will not forget you. Behold, I have engraved you on the palms of my hands; your walls are continually before me." (Isaiah 49:15–16)

How often have we looked at an unreturned call or an unanswered text message and asked the question, "What's wrong with me?" The enemy loves nothing more than to mess around with our imaginations. Think about it. How often have we sat alone, trying to understand why we were rejected? We analyze and overanalyze, trying to figure out what is the glaring flaw that caused the friend to withdraw, instead of addressing the issue honestly and head-on.

When we are abandoned without explanation, the message seems crystal clear: we're the kind of person who deserves to be abandoned...But this is not true. The Lord tells us that He will never abandon us. In fact, even when we are the ones who leave Him, just as the disciples did, it is He who stays faithful. He went to the cross just to save our relationship with Him. Let the crucifix always be that testament that you are worthy of pursuit by the God who will always show up for you.

And even if we played a part in the rupture of a friendship, redemption is always possible. Jesus always speaks the truth in love to us. It is His kindness that leads us to repentance and reminds us that He will finish the good work that He started in us. To follow Him fully is to increasingly become better at relationships, to become a better friend.

No matter what, God sees you from His perspective when He looks at you. To Him, you are worth the grave. He could never abandon you, for you are carved on the palm of His hand.

Take some time today to let God tell you exactly how He sees you. Let Him reveal to you just how far He has gone to get to your heart.

Day Four
GOSSIP

We've all been there. While enjoying the company of a group of friends, the subject turns to a woman who is not there. Before anyone can stop it, we've spent an hour deep in a gossip session. We know we shouldn't do it. We have experienced its destruction. Why is it so difficult to avoid, even though we know better? Why is it that other people's business and reputation are so intriguing to us? Words can breathe life or destroy hearts. The Lord created the world with a word. He knows just how powerful words are, and He has left us clear teaching on how and when we are to speak. These teachings from Scripture, if followed, will guard our friendships from strife and give them room to flourish.

1. Read James 3:3–10.

A. To what does Saint James compare the tongue in verses 3–5? Why does He make this comparison?

B. What two things come out of our mouth according to verse 9? Does that matter? See verse 10.

2. How we speak strongly affects the development of our character and the caliber of friendships we will pursue. What do the following Bible verses have to teach us about the power of our words?

A. According to Proverbs 18:21, over what two things does the tongue have power?

B. What can be rendered worthless if one does not control his tongue according to James 1:26?

C. Who utters slander according to Proverbs 10:18–19?

D. Proverbs 16:28 says, "A perverse man spreads strife and a whisperer separates close friends." How does being a whisperer relate to gossip?

E. Read Proverbs 18:8. To what are the words of a whisperer compared, and why?

F. As you reflect on these verses, can you think of any times recently that your words have been destructive rather than life-giving?

Gossip is a tremendously appealing temptation—even though it is wrong, it feels great at the time. It's human nature. But we have to remember, when we gossip, we make fools of ourselves, we cause dissension, and undermine our faith. Worst of all, gossip unleashes a story full of half-truths, at best, that can never be taken back once said. These stories tend to stick around, lodging themselves into the hearts and minds of those who hear them. There is no way to fully assess the damage that gossip causes. As women, we know gossip well. Our reputation for gossip has a long, earned history. We know what it's like when gossip devastates our hearts and our friendships. When we fail to watch what we say, everybody loses.

3. Have you ever been the subject of gossip that got back to you? If so, how did it make you feel? Reflect on what happened below.

4. Read Luke 6:45. What ultimately affects how we speak?

Our words are the fruit of the treasure in our hearts. When the bitter fruits of anger, resentment, discontent, unforgiveness, and insecurity lodge themselves in our hearts, gossip becomes an option that might make us feel better. We mistakenly think that someone else's failures negate our own. We revel in "being in the know" because it will make us feel important. We might believe the lie that focusing on the calamities in another person's life makes our own lives somehow happier. Embracing this lie, even when we aren't doing it intentionally, can cause the destructive habit of gossip to form.

Our hearts are meant to hold our brokenness, at least for a time. It is crucial to feel our feelings. The problem occurs when we let them fester. Untended hearts are more likely to resort to gossip. Even if we are trying to avoid gossip, our speech will be meaningless and our true intentions will eventually bubble to the surface if we don't address the issues in our hearts. We must bring all of the pain in our hearts to God. We must let Him lead us to do the work that will weed out the bad fruits and replace them with confidence, contentment, and self-control. When we have full hearts, we have courage to rejoice in the gifts of others and direct conversation away from gossip.

5. What is it that tempts you to gossip about your friends? Take a moment to identify what is going on in your heart. What are you trying to accomplish through gossip?

6. Ephesians 4:29 tells us that we should only speak what is edifying to the occasion and imparts grace. Colossians 4:6 tells us that our speech should be gracious and seasoned with salt. What three points of advice can we glean from James 1:19 on how to accomplish this type of speech?

In our culture of constant chatter and talking heads, the posture of simply listening almost seems foreign. However, the practice of listening is key to controlling our speech. Listening leads to empathy, to the understanding that people are complicated. If we listen, we are more likely to conclude that they deserve our mercy over our judgement. Being quick to listen and slow to speak also allows us to pay attention to the movements of our hearts. If we are having a negative reaction, or are itching to make a case against someone, we can take a moment to prayerfully invite wisdom into our choices. We can make better decisions about what to say and when to say it. We can invite the direction of the Holy Spirit into any conversation, which will leave us with fewer regrets. Make no mistake, it takes a courageous woman to avoid gossip. Idle talk is all around us. Being the woman who stays silent or changes the subject can feel awkward or overly pious. But your friend's reputation and your own peace of heart are worth protecting. Step up and defend her. You could say something like, "I just don't feel comfortable talking about her when she isn't here to shed light on this." What will result? Awkwardness? Definitely. But something else will come of it, too. People will think twice about drawing you into these kinds of conversations in the future. What a relief!

Quiet your heart and enjoy His presence… Jesus, be at the center of our speech.

"Set a guard over my mouth, O Lord, keep watch over the door of my lips!" (Psalm 141:3)

Venerable Archbishop Fulton Sheen, well known for his 1950's show, Life is Worth Living, *recorded stories of his life in his autobiography,* Treasure in Clay. *He tells of a time when there was a feud going on between a professor and the Bishop at the school where Sheen taught. Sheen found himself in the middle of the argument which caused him to be moved from the school of theology to the school of philosophy. Months later, secretary of state to the Vatican, Cardinal Pacelli, asked Sheen about the incident. Knowing that this was his chance to exonerate himself, Sheen could have gossiped about the Bishop. Instead, he responded, "Your Eminence, I beg to be excused from any comment about the university or its rector (the Bishop)." After that conversation, the Bishop was moved from the school to a different diocese. His silence revealed his character which eventually led to the truth.*[20]

Sheen revealed the level of his character when he had the courage to stay silent rather than speak poorly of another to exonerate himself. Make no mistake, it takes a woman of the same type of courage to avoid gossip when idle talk is a constant temptation. The middle school desire to fit in has never left most of us and sometimes gossip seems to help bond us to other women. It is never worth it. Female friendships would take on a whole new life and reputation if we would simply quit gossiping about one another.

Lord, transform our hearts and guard our speech. Make our words a source of life in our friendships.

Day Five
JEALOUSY

When jealousy reigns in friendships, neither woman is free to be herself. Joy between them is stunted. Discontentment and competition lurk in the background of every conversation. Of course, the opportunities for comparison and jealousy to enter into relationships are at an all-time high. We are no longer just trying to keep up with our immediate circle of friends. Social media has made it possible for us to scroll through an infinite amount of highlight reels from other women. While scrolling we see a picture of an acquaintance on vacation followed by pictures of good friends hanging out without us. We may also scroll past a woman with smiling kids in a pristine home or a stunning scene from the life of a celebrity. We can falsely assess convincing evidence that other women are better off than we are. Most of us can attest to the quote attributed to Teddy Roosevelt, "Comparison is the thief of joy." If you spend any time on social media without grounding **your** heart in Him, it's easy to feel miserable. Jesus wants us to have complete joy. If we are to live joyfully, then there is no place for jealousy.

---

20 Archbishop Fulton Sheen, *Treasures in Clay* (New York: Crown Publishing Group, 2009), 48.

1.   "Comparison" and "jealousy" can be synonymous with envy.

    A.   What does envy do according to Proverbs 14:3?

    B.   What else do you find where you find envy, according to James 3:14–16?

While fleeting feelings of comparison are natural, there is a type of jealousy that seeps into the core of our being. The image of envy rotting our bones is a graphic one. It is the perfect description of what happens to us when jealousy takes over in a friendship. Envy eats away at our own inner goodness and ability to be good to others. We shift our focus away from what we do have to the many things that others have. Our gratitude turns into entitlement. We pine for what others have—a beautiful house, a different job, a great body—reminding ourselves of why we deserve more than we have. At best, we feel inadequate. At worst, we turn into people who secretly smirk when others fail. When we're focused on what others have, we are blinded to all the good in our own lives.

2.   Write about your experience with comparison and jealousy below. Have you seen either of these feelings affect your friendships? If so, how? How do you deal with your own feelings of comparison and jealousy?

3.   In Luke 15:11–24 Jesus tells the parable of the prodigal son. A man had two sons. The younger of the two asked his father for his inheritance early, and his father agreed. The son took the inheritance and squandered it on a sinful life. When he had nothing left, he hired himself out as a servant. While feeding the pigs, he realized that his father's servants were treated better than he was. He decided to return to his father and ask to be hired as a servant. When the father saw his son approach the house, he ran to him. The father kissed his son. He put sandals on his feet, and a ring on his finger. He then killed the fattened calf and threw a party.

    A.   Read Luke 15:25–32. How did the older brother respond?

B. What was the father's response to the older son?

C. Why do you think the older son reacted this way? Can you relate? Reflect below.

The older son was jealous of his younger brother when he saw how his father celebrated the younger son. He knew his brother had betrayed the family and spent all of his inheritance. Yet, their father rejoiced when he came back. Having been loyal for so many years, the older brother felt as though his father was holding out on him. He had missed the fact that everything his father owned was his all along. He felt so jealous, he couldn't see what was right in front of him.

Imbedded in jealousy is the scarcity mentality: the belief that there is not enough of God's goodness to go around. When we ascribe to this belief, we look at our own gifts with disdain. We convince ourselves that our gifts are not as good as someone else's gifts. We then foster in our hearts a spirit of ingratitude. When we are focused on what God has given other women, we become blind to what He has given to us. We forget how He wants to use our gifts in the world. Resentment starts to build and our friendships begin to suffer.

4. Read Ephesians 2:8–10. Why does Saint Paul say that no one can boast and for what does it say we were created to do?

5. The details of our lives look different. We differ in looks, lifestyle, family size, wealth, and life circumstances. However, the most important thing in the universe, the Gospel of Jesus Christ, is offered to us all. Each of us stands before God as a sinner with empty hands. He offers us the gift of His salvation, to live forever with Him. No one has been left out of that promise. What happens to us when we accept this promise and are baptized in Christ? What happens when we belong to Christ? See Galatians 3:26–29.

6. Take a moment and reflect on the gifts that God has given to you.

    A. List them below and thank God for these things—the people, the opportunities, the possessions, and even the challenges.

    B. Now, write out the gifts that you see in other women's lives. Thank God for them as well and ask Him to give you a heart that rejoices in others.

Quiet your heart and enjoy His presence. . . When we are content in God, our jealousy fades away.

1 Thessalonians 5:18 says "Give thanks in all circumstances; for this is God's will for you in Christ Jesus." It is God's will for us that we find a way to be grateful in all circumstances for what He has given to us. Anytime we follow God's will, we take one more step in becoming who we were meant to be.

Focusing on gratitude does not mean we should gloss over the bad things in our lives and emit false positivity. The Lord calls us to always be looking for His hand in our lives, recognizing that we have been given everything that we need to live joyfully and fulfill our unique purpose. In this grateful disposition, we are guarded from the lasting effects of jealousy as we continually return to God's throne with thanksgiving. We can then be women who can genuinely "rejoice with those who rejoice" (Romans 12:15) from a place of confidence, contentment and love for others.

Conclusion

Katie and Maria had become dear friends. They spent a ton of time together, had been in each other's weddings, and had supported one another through their first pregnancies. Katie thought that she and Maria shared a deep, committed friendship.

Out of the blue, Maria excluded Katie from one of her life's biggest events. There was no explanation. Katie felt hurt and rejected. I could hear the resentment in Katie's voice as she told me about it.

About a month after the crack in their friendship had formed, Katie and I went on a walk. I knew the subject of her friendship with Maria would eventually surface. She didn't say what I was expecting. "Maria and I caught up over coffee" she began, "...and I apologized to her."

"Oh, you did?" I asked, trying not to sound surprised.

"Yes. I told her that I had been angry with her for months, but I realized that I wasn't even considering what she was going through. I asked her to forgive me for harboring a grudge against her, and she forgave me."

"Wow," I responded, "that was incredibly mature of you."

Our conversation about Maria ended there, but Katie's decision to approach Maria with a spirit of humility and repentance had a major impact on me. Katie and Maria's friendship had been headed towards a silent end. Maria was overwhelmed, pushing people away, and Katie was hurt. Instead of giving into secret resentment, anger, and gossip, Katie chose reconciliation. Her choice to approach her dear friend to ask for forgiveness revealed the maturity of Katie's character. While some friendships are beyond repair and need to end for the sake of each woman, Katie's story teaches us an important lesson. More often than not, these barriers to friendship can be overcome if only we have the courage to make a move towards reconciliation.

Each of us is a work in progress. We have all made mistakes and behaved badly in our relationships. When we have been the ones to cause hurt, we should humble ourselves and ask for forgiveness. Even if the other person will not forgive, God can heal a repentant heart. His mercy awaits us if only we ask.

We have all stewed in the mess and hurts of our friendships when we were called to grow in maturity and walk forward through the challenges. Thank goodness that we serve a God who is slow to anger and abounding in kindness. Regardless of our failures, God has given us all that we need to become more like Him. He will equip us to handle our friendships with grace. He has a vision of who we can be. He has a vision for who our friends can be. He wants to use our friendships to help us get there. He can build in us the level of maturity that we need to live out healthy friendships. With His grace, we can grow in friendships characterized by joy, patience, honesty, and a vision of the good of the other.

Are you not there yet? Take heart. He who started a good work in you will finish it.[21] He hasn't given up on you, so press on. Don't quit.

---

21 Philippians 1:6.

"Not that I have already obtained this or am already perfect; but I press on to make it my own, because Christ Jesus has made me his own…forgetting what lies behind and straining forward to what lies ahead, I press on toward the goal for the prize of the upward call of God in Christ Jesus." (Philippians 3:12-14)

Want to learn more about this week's topic? Don't miss Lesson 3's short video from Mallory at walkingwithpurpose.com/videos.

My Resolution

In what specific way will I apply what I learned in this lesson?

Examples:

1. I will consider my own behavior in my friendships this week and answer the following questions:

   Am I acting in a mature and healthy way?

   How is my behavior serving as a barrier to my friendships?

   I will write these down and bring them to prayer asking God to give me the next steps to overcome these behaviors.

2. Is there a friendship in my life that has some slow leaks? If so, I will approach my friend in humility and ask forgiveness for the part I may be playing.

3. I will spend time in the chapel asking the Lord to give me a vision for who my friends could be at their best. I will write these down and use them as a foundation to pray for my friends.

My Resolution:

NOTES

NOTES

 NOTES

Lesson 4

MOVING PAST THE PAIN

Introduction

The history of the Israelite nation, God's chosen people, is full of pain. They were at war with many nations, they were exiled from their homeland multiple times, and their city was completely destroyed—more than once. Each time, God came to their rescue. Then the Israelites had to begin the process of restoring what was lost.

Almost 500 years before Jesus was born, the Israelites returned to Jerusalem after fifty years of exile in Babylon. When they arrived at their homeland, their temple, their culture, and their wall were all in ruins. The Old Testament book of Nehemiah tells the story of Nehemiah, the Israelite cupbearer to the king of Persia whom God called away from his post and back to Jerusalem. His task was to rebuild the wall so that the city would once again flourish in safety.

In Nehemiah 2:11–16, Nehemiah traveled around the wall to assess the damage that left Jerusalem vulnerable to attack for years. He rode around the city to see parts of the wall breached and gates that were consumed by fire. After he did this, he spoke to men who would rebuild the wall:

> Then I said to them, "You see the trouble we are in, how Jerusalem lies in ruins with its gates burned. Come, let us build the wall of Jerusalem, that we may no longer suffer disgrace." And I told them of the hand of my God which had been upon me for good, and also of the words which the king had spoken to me. And they said, "Let us rise up and build." So they strengthened their hands for good work. (Nehemiah 2:17–18)

We have already established that women's friendships can be a battlefield. No one gets out unscathed. Like Nehemiah, we must assess the damages. When we do this, however, we cannot just sit in the ruins. We cannot allow ourselves to be overcome with pain and anger. We have to do the work of restoration. This work begins in our own hearts and minds. If we fail to do hard work, our wounds will only get worse with time.

If we turn to Him for renewal, He will fortify our minds. Graciously, He will give us insight into how He sees the person on the other side of our pain. If we learn to walk in His ways, we will gain the skills that are necessary to protect our hearts and friendships in the future.

Let's begin the work of rebuilding with God at our side, so we can enter our friendships with healed spirits and open hearts.

"Our work is scattered and extensive, and we are widely separated from one another along the wall; wherever you hear the trumpet sound, join us there; our God will fight for us." (Nehemiah 4:13-15)

Day One
UNDERSTANDING LONELINESS

In a survey taken in January 2020, six out of ten people said they feel left out, poorly understood, or are lacking companionship.[22] That was **before** the pandemic placed the whole world on lock down. Loneliness is a feeling all experience. Some of us handle it through entertainment and distraction, but ultimately, most of us look to our relationships for a respite from loneliness. We think that the right romance or the perfect friendship will quell the empty feelings in our hearts. Those relationships always come up short. God allows this gnawing feeling of loneliness so that we seek Him. He understands what it means to feel alone, and He has shown us how to handle it.

1. In Lesson 2, we saw that God created us to live in a perfect relationship with Him and with others. When sin entered the picture, everything went haywire.

   Read Romans 1:21–25.

   A. What happened when man refused to glorify God or give Him thanks according to verses 21 and 22?

---

[22] "Cigna Takes Action To Combat The Rise Of Loneliness And Improve Mental Wellness In America," Cigna, 01/03/2020, https://www.cigna.com/newsroom/news-releases/2020/cigna-takes-action-to-combat-the-rise-of-loneliness-and-improve-mental-wellness-in-america.

B. What exchange did they make? What did they choose to worship in verse 25?

What is the lie that humanity embraced? William Barclay, a renowned theologian, explored this verse in his commentary, *The Letter to the Romans*. In it, Barclay explained that man embraced the lie that man's will is more important than God's will. He wrote, "They found their standards in their own opinions and not in the laws of God. They lived in a self-centered instead of a God centered universe."[23] Man embraced the lie that the self was to be glorified over God, and so they chose to worship what they thought would bring themselves glory instead of worshipping God for the sake of His glory. We participate in this lie every time we disobey God, every time we think that our way will make us happier than His way.

2. What effect did sin, our acceptance of the lie, have on our human relationships? See CCC 1872.

Loneliness is the feeling we get when we realize that we will never be fully known, fully loved, and fully understood in this life, no matter how great our relationships may be. That feeling will never completely go away. It comes from our injured relationships and is the direct result of the original sin. This ever-present emptiness, however, prompts us to seek God. Only He can fill the longings of our hearts. While the relationships we form are good and do bring us a certain level of fulfillment, they are all meant to lead us to God. He's the only one who can bring complete rest to our hearts.

3. How do you deal with loneliness? Have you ever counted on someone to bring you total fulfillment and learned that they couldn't? Write about that experience.

The loneliness we experience stems from the fact that we are born into a fallen world, but that isn't the end of the story. The tough news of the Gospel is, "all have sinned and fall short of the glory of God" (Romans 3:23) and "the wages of sin is death" (Romans

---

23 William Barclay, *The Letter to the Romans* (Westminster John Knox Press: Louisville, KY, 2017), 33.

6:23). But Jesus didn't leave us there. Romans 6:23 goes on to say, "the free gift of God is eternal life in Christ Jesus our Lord." He defeated death through His resurrection and gave us new life. 2 Corinthians 5:17 says, "Therefore, if anyone is in Christ, the new creation has come: The old has gone, the new is here!"

The *Catechism of the Catholic Church* tells us in CCC 405, "Baptism, by imparting the life of Christ's grace, erases original sin and turns a man back towards God, but the consequences for nature, weakened and inclined to evil, persist in man and summon him to spiritual battle."

We will only experience total fulfillment in heaven when we finally experience complete union with Him. While we are on earth, we must live with the earthly consequences of sin. We can accept that we must deal with our loneliness instead of trying to ignore it or expecting others to fill it. We have a choice regarding what we do with this feeling.

4. Read Matthew 26:36–44.

   A. Why does Jesus say He is going to pray in verse 38?

   B. To whom did Jesus turn to in this hour of desperate need?
       See verses 39 and 42.

   C. Were that apostles able to give Jesus adequate support?
       See verses 40–41 and 43–44.

Jesus experienced a level of loneliness that we will never experience. Can you imagine being a sinless person in a world dominated by sin? Can you imagine developing friendships with those who you came to save, knowing they would betray you? Jesus was fully aware that His friendships were not the foundation of His fulfillment. His fulfillment came from His relationship with His Father. Leading up to the darkest hour of His life, Jesus did not hide from God, nor did He surrender to loneliness. He admitted the state of His soul and went to the Father for comfort. He invited His friends along for support but did not depend on them for the comfort that they couldn't provide.

In these moments, Jesus practiced solitude, a disposition of being alone that is a far cry from loneliness. Loneliness is marked by the negative feeling of isolation, but solitude is marked by communion with God. When we are lonely, we can allow ourselves to be overcome with the feeling of abandonment and desolation; in solitude, we are not alone—God is wooing us to Himself. When we are in solitude, we can speak with God honestly and let Him work in our souls, trusting that He is present.

5. Think about your own feelings of loneliness. How can you turn to God for fulfillment in those moments when your earthly relationships are not enough to quiet your loneliness?

Quiet your heart and enjoy His presence… He is with you in the waiting.

What would it have been like to be David when he was a shepherd? What would it be like to hear only the noise of nature? He spent day after day alone in the wilderness, and He became "a man after God's own heart." All those nights under the sky laid the foundation for his future.

We honor true friendship when we lean into God—the only One who can truly satisfy. The fullness of that satisfaction will only happen in heaven, but while we wait, He is here. Meditate on the words of David from Psalm 16 below. How will you keep your eyes on the Lord? Even on your most lonely day, He has not abandoned you. Allow Him to fill you with the joy of His presence. He has given you relationships as a foretaste of the eternal pleasure that awaits.

> *I keep my eyes always on the Lord. With him at my right hand, I will not be shaken. Therefore my heart is glad and my tongue rejoices; my body also will rest secure, because you will not abandon me to the realm of the dead, nor will you let your faithful one see decay. You make known to me the path of life; you will fill me with joy in your presence, with eternal pleasures at your right hand. (Psalm 16:8-11)*

Day Two
IT MAY NOT BE ABOUT YOU

When friendships go awry, it's not long before we start replaying the stories in our minds. We think of everything we could have done wrong and all the bad things that our friends must be saying about us. If we aren't careful, we start making up conversations that deem us innocent and others guilty.

When we engage in this thinking, we make the situation about us. We spin a reality in our heads that leaves no room for understanding what the other person may be experiencing. As Christians, we are called to see the world as it is meant to be seen, with God at the center, and others as more important than ourselves. When we focus on God, our feelings are no longer the most important part of the problem. Freedom can be restored to our friendships.

1. Read Genesis 11:1–4.

    A. What did the people say in verse 4?

    B. Genesis 11 is the story of the Tower of Babel. The people of Babel desired a name for themselves so they began to build an enormous tower. God saw their progress, confused their language, and scattered them across the earth to keep them from completing the project. In the very next chapter, Abram appears on the scene and meets God. What does the Lord tell him in Genesis 12:1–2?

    C. Genesis 11:4 and Genesis 12:1 both claim that man's name will be made great. What is the difference between these two claims?

The people in Genesis 11 sought to make a name for themselves, and they turned their focus away from God. They were completely self-centered. The story was about them. Consequently, God opposed their pride.

Abram's behavior in Genesis 12 was different. He did not grasp after his own greatness. God declared that He would make Abram's name great, and Abram followed His lead. Shortly after He made this promise, God told Abram to go outside and look up to the heavens where He vowed to make his descendants as many as the stars in the sky (Genesis 15). Abram's eyes were turned upward, focused on the glory and greatness of God. He humbly accepted this blessing, recognizing that he was not the center of the story. Through Abram's humility, the story of salvation progressed and generations were blessed. Abram eventually becomes Abraham, the father of Judaism, Christianity, and Islam.

Genesis 11 and Genesis 12 lay before us two ways that we can choose to live. We can live centered on ourselves, or we can live centered on God. The first way makes everything about us and makes sure that everyone else is focused on us. The second way makes everything about God and His people.

2. Pride can be defined as an excessive focus on self. Pride reaches the heights of self-exaltation and the depths of self-deprecation. Many of us battle with the highs and lows of pride on a daily basis. Reflect below on how you struggle with pride. How does your pride affect your friendships?

3. C.S. Lewis said that "Humility is not thinking less of yourself, but it is thinking of yourself less."

   A. How does Saint Paul say we should think of ourselves according to Romans 12:3?

   B. How does Philippians 2:3—4 direct us to consider others?

4. Humility is more than a disposition of our hearts and minds. It should show in the way we live. List out, according to 1 Peter 3:8—12, the ways we should or shouldn't be conducting ourselves in our relationships with others.

5. How does Romans 12:18 say that we should seek to live? Is this always possible?

The Lord commands us to do everything we can on our part to foster healthy relationships. We may do everything right in a friendship and things may still go wrong. Friends suffer tragedies that make them emotionally unavailable. They go through life changes that keep them busy. They deal with their own insecurities and pride. These factors may affect our friendships, but they may not be about us.

We can tell ourselves all the stories in the world, but the state of the friendship may be out of our control. When things go sideways, we must resist the temptation to make it about us and our comfort. Instead, we should search our hearts honestly. Have we acted uprightly? Have we done something for which we need to ask forgiveness? If so, we ask for forgiveness and give grace in return. If we have acted in good faith, we should set ourselves free from overthinking the situation. In those moments, we can humbly offer support and then let God do the work.

6. Have you ever invented a saga all about what you had done wrong in a friendship, only to learn that the situation had nothing to do with you? What did you learn from that experience? How can you apply that lesson in future friendships?

Quiet your heart and enjoy His presence… He must increase, we must decrease.

There is a good chance that you have heard or seen the verses John 3:16 somewhere in modern culture—social media, a billboard, a hand-lettered sign. "For God so loved the world that he gave his only-begotten Son, that whoever believes in him should not perish but have eternal life." All of human history is centered around one event: the life, death, and resurrection of Jesus. Why did God do this? Yes, it is partly because He loves us and wants us to be in heaven with Him, but there is a deeper reason. God repeatedly tells His people throughout Scripture that He did not rescue us because we are great. He rescues because He is great. We are not the point. God is the center of the story and all creation exists to give Him praise.

This should be the best news in the world to us. If we are not the point of history, we can breathe more deeply. You are not the point—believe it and breathe! We will live life less offended, which will change the tone of our relationships. When we live as if it's all about us, we enter every relationship with expectations. When those expectations aren't met, anger and resentment enter the scene. Others didn't act the way we want them to act. When we are centered on God, all of the sudden there is more room for grace, forgiveness and humility because it was never about us to begin with. The way "they" act isn't about us at all.

1 Corinthians 10:31 says, "So, whether you eat or drink, or whatever you do, do all to the glory of God." How would our lives change if we made God the center of everything? How would this change our friendships? Each person would feel freer to be themselves. Quarrels and conflicts would be resolved more quickly. In the midst of hard times, we will be able to pursue the truth of the matter and allow God to be glorified in our disposition toward each other.

Day Three
RECOGNIZING TOXIC FRIENDSHIPS

In Lesson 3, we learned about the behaviors in friendship that keep us from developing healthy, life-giving friendships. Each of us is prone to those behaviors on any given day. It is normal to struggle with gossip, jealousy, and broken trust. Feelings get hurt. Most of the time, these behaviors cause minor to moderate problems and can be overcome through proper communication and forgiveness. Sometimes, these behaviors become the main focus of a friendship. The consequences of jealousy, gossip, and other bad behaviors change the very nature of a relationship and continually harm the spirit of one or both women involved. The friendship has become toxic. We have to act against this. We must reconsider the role that the person plays in our lives. How do we spot a toxic friendship, and what do we do when we have recognized the problems?

1. What advice do the following Bible verses give us about how we should choose our friends?

    A. Proverbs 22:24–25

    B. Proverbs 13:20

C. Proverbs 14:7

D. 1 Corinthians 15:33

2. Scripture supports the notion that the character of the people we spend time with will impact us—for good or for bad. Our friendships will either help us move toward or away from the good. So how do we know the difference between a friendship that is going through a rough patch and a friendship that has become toxic?

Consider the presence of some of these red flags:

Constant Drama: Incessant drama is toxic. High drama results when a woman is always at odds with others, consistently complaining about how she was victimized, or causing dissension through gossip or a combative attitude. Where there was peace, her behavior introduces chaos. At first, high drama friendships are entertaining. There is always a great story. But constant dissention is exhausting. It inhibits the growth of joy and maturity between friends.

A. The Bible calls us to live in such a way that guards against drama and its negative effects. Describe how we are called to live according to 1 Thessalonians 4:11–12.

Codependency: There are two types of codependency. One involves attachment to someone with an addiction. Discussing this type of codependency is beyond the scope of this study. If you think this might be your situation, counseling can be immensely helpful. The other type occurs when one or both members of the friendship depend on the other for total validation of their personal worth and decisions. When someone is codependent on someone else, it is difficult for them to make even small decisions without the approval of that specific person. This results in constant, inappropriate amounts of communication and the inability to make decisions without the opinion of the other. Codependent relationships keep each woman from standing confidently in her identity and her unique gifts to the world.

B. While friends should be able to rely on each other to a certain degree, who is ultimately responsible for our work and decisions according to Galatians 6:4–5? Who will be with us when we eventually stand before God?

Ultra-Self-Focused: A friend who is ultra-self-focused is unable to respond properly to the other's needs in the friendship because she is consumed with herself. There are times when a woman may be going through something that requires her life to be the main topic of conversation. But if she never asks a question that isn't about her, the relationship isn't reciprocal. If she is unable to focus on the needs of her friend and manipulates all situations to be about her, the relationship has become toxic.

C. Read Ephesians 5:21 and write out the verse below. How does this direction keep friendships from becoming all about one person?

Our modern sentiments may be offended by submitting to another person. Most of us don't like the idea of submitting to anyone. With this passage Saint Paul is directing us back to the words of Jesus when He said, "Love one another as I have loved you." How did Jesus love us? He laid down His life for us. He placed our wellbeing above His own. Relationships centered on Christ are marked by this "others first" attitude. When we all submit to each other, everyone's needs are met. If a member of the friendship makes herself the sole focus and beneficiary of the relationship, it may be time to re-evaluate that relationship. The truth is, this kind of relationship isn't really helping her, either.

Demeaning: Comparison and spurts of jealousy will creep into our relationships, but the dysfunction escalates when a friend can never rejoice in the other's good fortune. In Christ-like friendships, we should be building each other up. There is no room for degradation. If a friend cannot say good things about the other but instead is constantly magnifying the other person's flaws and mistakes, the relationship is toxic. Additionally, the relationship has become toxic if one woman finds herself hiding her joys and successes because she knows that it will only cause her friend to react poorly and belittle or try to one up her.

D. In Lesson 2, Day Four, we established that our words have the power to build up or tear down. According to Ephesians 4:29, how are we to use our speech?

3. Reflecting on the red flags listed previously, have you ever experienced a toxic friendship? Write about your experience below. Name the behavior that dominated your friendship. How did it affect you, the other woman, and your friendship? Was it resolved? If so, how?

4. Handling a toxic friendship can be extremely difficult. We don't want to cause drama or hurt feelings.

A. How should we handle contentious relationships according to Matthew 18:15–17?

Jesus did not tell His disciples in Matthew 18 to immediately drop someone who sins against us. He also didn't tell us to share a litany of our complaints to another friend when someone else hurts us. We are to first approach our friend directly and privately. If that sounds intimidating to you, you are not alone. This kind of confrontation can be a healing step in a relationship, but it takes courage, wisdom, and prayer. It is always best to do this face-to-face with your friend.

B. Why does Saint Paul say we should avoid foolish controversies in Titus 3:9–11? How should we approach someone who stirs up division?

Saint Paul did not say that we should allow bad behavior to stir up strife and steal our peace over and over again. We should not withhold forgiveness, but we are not required to give ourselves over to a pattern of toxic behaviors. Healing and restoration can happen, but there is a process. Fortunately, that process is outlined in Scripture and does not turn us into doormats. We should always seek

God's wisdom and the counsel of other holy people when deciding how to move forward with a toxic relationship. If the toxic friendship does not change after direct conversations and attempts at restoration, however, it may be necessary to walk away, for your sake and for hers.

5.   In a recent conversation I had with a counselor, she mentioned that she directs her clients to categorize their friendships into concentric circles. The middle circle is reserved for intimate friends, the next circle is for good friends, and the outer circle is for acquaintances. When she speaks to her clients about toxic friendships, she asks them to place that relationship somewhere in their circles. She then asks her client to consider where the friendship should be. If a friendship is toxic, it is possible that reprioritizing the friendship is appropriate. If a friendship has become toxic, maybe it's time to move it from a "good friend" status to an "acquaintance." If the friendship would still have a deeply negative impact, she walks them through distancing themselves from the friendship altogether. In Appendix 3, in the back of the study, there is a copy of these circles and directions for reflecting on your friendships. Take a moment to reflect on each of your friendships and which circle they occupy. Are they where they should be? Read Appendix 3 and share your reflections here.

Quiet your heart and enjoy His presence. . . Darkness will not overcome.

"Be sober, be watchful. Your adversary the devil prowls around like a roaring lion, seeking someone to devour." (1 Peter 5:8)

The devil wants to destroy us. He hates healthy relationships because he knows that they form us into women who more closely resemble our Creator, his real enemy. The more he can twist our hearts and our behaviors, the more toxic our relationships will become. This is what he wants, and we should not forget it. Even when the darkness is so black that it seems we will not find our way through, Jesus always shows up. He is the light that shines through the darkness and He wins every time.

We may not be able to change the heart of a friend but our Lord is always ready, waiting to change us. He untwists what is twisted. He heals what is broken. If we give Him our hearts of stone, He will turn them into hearts of flesh. How does He do this? By giving us His Holy Spirit. How do we know that we are living in the Spirit? There will be evidence in our lives.

Galatians 5:19–24 lays out the fruits of darkness and the fruits of the Spirit:

> *Darkness brings dysfunction, the Spirit brings health. One brings chaos; the other brings peace. Now the works of the flesh are plain: immorality, impurity, licentiousness, idolatry, sorcery, enmity, strife, jealousy, anger, selfishness, dissension, party spirit, envy, drunkenness, carousing, and the like. I warn you, as I warned you before, that those who do such things shall not inherit the kingdom of God. But the fruit of the Spirit is love, joy, peace, patience, kindness, goodness, faithfulness, gentleness, self-control; against such there is no law. And those who belong to Christ Jesus have crucified the flesh with its passions and desires.*

Life with Christ offers an end to the toxicity in our own hearts. In applying His wisdom and the good counsel of His saints to our lives, we gain the tools needed to walk away from toxic behavior and toward greater relational health.

Day Four
SETTING BOUNDARIES

The term "boundaries" has become popular over the past decade. We hear the word often and are told that we need to be better at keeping boundaries in our lives, but what exactly are boundaries. According to the book *Boundaries*, "They define us. They define what is me and what is not me. A boundary shows me where I end and someone else begins, leading me to a sense of ownership."[24] In other words, boundaries help us to understand and preserve who we are.

1. Healthy boundaries allow us to protect our God-given identities and reject anything that contradicts what He says about us.

   A. Read 2 Corinthians 5:17. Between what two things did Saint Paul establish a boundary?

   B. According to Proverbs 4:23, why should we have boundaries around our hearts?

---

24 Dr. Henry Cloud and Dr. John Townsend, *Boundaries* (Michigan: Zondervan, 1992), 29.

C. Saint Paul commands us to establish another boundary in Colossians 3:1–2. What is it?

By Jesus' cross, death, and resurrection, He set a boundary between who we were and who we *are*. He offered us a new life, a new identity, a new heart and a new mind. The enemy wants nothing more than for us to turn back to who we were. He will do everything he can to make sure that we forget our identities, neglect our hearts, and desert the formation of our minds. Setting good boundaries helps us to guard and nurture these core parts of us against the enemy. Then, God cultivates our characters for Himself.

When we fail to set up boundaries in our friendships, confusion can easily set in. The truth about who we are and the role we play in the friendship becomes blurred. For example, if a woman in a friendship never speaks her mind or asserts her preferences, the expectation is that she will always do what the other friend wants. This woman becomes the giver and the other the taker. These roles are disordered—each woman is supposed to contribute to the friendship. Or one friend might have a habit of doing things last minute and end up in mini crises that requires assistance. Her friend is willing to step in and help but starts to feel resentful when the procrastination becomes a pattern. In this instance, the friendship becomes one of use and enabling instead of mutual contribution. The friendship should be an opportunity for both women to grow in virtue, one by planning ahead and the other by helping from a place of freedom. Boundaries make this possible. If the resentful friend had wisely set a boundary at the start, saying something like, "I am happy to help when I can, but I always need three days lead time in order to plan," the other friend would likely have respected that and the friendship wouldn't suffer.

2. Is there a time that you failed to establish boundaries in your friendships? How did that failure harm you or your friend? Write about your experience below.

3. If we make healthy boundaries a habit, they can protect our friendships from toxicity and keep our relationships honest and thriving. Throughout Jesus' time on earth, He was constantly establishing and living according to healthy boundaries. He is the perfect example of how we can do this in our own lives. Let's look at some of the boundaries He set in the Gospels.

A. What wisdom did Jesus give regarding what we say in Matthew 5:37?

This is especially hard to do in our culture. Too often, we associate speaking our mind with being rude. We do not need to be rude to speak plainly, allowing our yes to mean yes and our no to mean no. Speaking plainly is a large part of speaking the truth in love (Ephesians 4:15). A simple response could be, "You know, that would be very hard for me to do right now, so I am going to need to say no, but feel free to ask me in the future." Be honest while still maintaining a warm demeanor. If you don't have the bandwidth for something, say no!

B. Did Jesus spend all of His time with others doing what they wanted Him to do? See Mark 6:46 and Luke 6:12.

C. Did Jesus perform miracles regardless of the disposition of others? See Mark 6:1–4.

The boundaries that Jesus set in His life were part of His character. His identity, His heart, and His mind were totally conformed to the will of God. He acted in freedom. He was assertive about the truth with others, He said "no" to others, He took time alone to decompress and be with His Father, and He refrained from giving into the demands of other people. He set the example for us to do the same. In this spirit, our relationships can thrive, we can repair the relationships that are going off track, and we can stand firm in the identity that God has given us.

4. Is there a friendship in your life right now that could use some boundaries? What behaviors can you implement that would set the friendship back on the right track? Write out some specific steps on how you can implement the boundaries needed in the friendship.

Quiet your heart and enjoy His presence… His path leads us to freedom.

While most of us love the concept of boundaries, few of us are good at setting and keeping them. There is something about the thought of drawing a line in the sand, saying no, or asserting our own needs that makes us bristle. Placing boundaries between us and others can feel mean. The word "no" rings cold when we want to be warm and friendly. Boundaries are not mean: they are a gift we can give to ourselves and other women. Properly established boundaries provide the space needed for each woman to thrive as an individual who is uniquely created and called by God.

Do you struggle with the idea of establishing boundaries in your own life? Take heart, a boundary is not a wall that is meant to keep everyone out and you in. Instead, a boundary is a filter. Through the filter of a healthy boundary, through prayer and counsel from wise friends, you decide how to let God's goodness into your friendships and how to keep the bad out. God calls you to protect what He has given to you for your sake and for that sake of others. Like most things in the Christian life, setting boundaries takes courage. Turn to Him, let Him speak over you and give you all that you need to establish the type of friendships that glorify Him.

Dear Lord,

Thank You for making me a new creation. Thank You for making me a gift to the other women in my life and for making them a gift to me. I ask You for the grace and the courage to establish healthy boundaries. Lord, You are my protection and I claim the words of Psalm 18:2 in your presence: "The Lord is my rock, and my fortress, and my deliverer, my God, my rock, in whom I take refuge; My shield, and the horn of my salvation, my stronghold." Give me the wisdom to establish boundaries and to honor the boundaries of others so that health and freedom would reign in my friendships and reflect Your glory to the world. Amen.

Day Five
FINDING FREEDOM IN FORGIVENESS

We can do all of the right things in our friendships and still find ourselves hurting. Many of us have experienced such deep wounds in friendship that genuine relationship and vulnerability seem impossible. Surface level relationships seem to serve us well. All the while, we carry the heavy burden of words that can't be unsaid and actions that can't be undone. Freedom from our burdens and healing from our hurts can only be found through forgiveness. While we know the concept of forgiveness, it seems to go against our deep desire for justice. Forgiveness can feel like a weakness rather than a path to freedom. God still commands us to forgive and, in His word, He tells us why.

1. Read Matthew 18:23–27.

    A. How much money did the servant owe the king? Would he be able to repay the debt? See verses 24 and 25.

    B. What did the servant ask of his master in verse 26?

    C. How did the master respond to the servant in verse 27? Did he ever have to pay back the loan?

A *talent* in Biblical times was a unit of measure that would have equaled about 6,000 denarii. One denarius was a day's wage.[25] This means that the servant in this parable owed the king 60,000,000 days' wages, an outrageous amount of money. It would have been impossible for the servant ever to pay it back and the king knew this. The only way to settle the debt was for the king to forgive the loan completely. The king alone was rich enough to cover the cost.

Jesus used a ridiculously large sum of money in the parable. He was driving home the point that we, in our sin, are completely helpless in front of a perfect God. Jesus' example of the king and the servant magnifies just how far God's compassion reaches.

2. How does each of the following Bible verses describe our sin and God's response to us?

    Psalm 103:10–12

    Romans 6:23

    Psalm 130:3–4

---

25 "Talent," Bible Study Tools, 9/29/2020, https://biblestudytools.com/dictionary/talent/.

The wages that we owe God for our sin far outweigh the servant's debt in the parable. There is no good work in existence that will make up for our disobedience to God. Instead of condemning us, however, Jesus stepped in and paid the price for our sin. Through the blood that He shed, He opened up the gates to God's mercy. We now have access to a relationship with Him. Through confessing our sins and accepting His forgiveness, we are freed from defining ourselves according to our shortcomings and our impossibly huge debts.

3. It is so important that we continually return to what God has to say about our sin and our need for His mercy. We live and breathe in a culture that has forgotten the seriousness of sin. Most people err on the side of letting themselves off the hook for their moral failings. Some of us habitually compare ourselves to those who are "worse" than us rather than comparing ourselves to God who is perfect. How do you see yourself and your sin? Do you recognize your need for mercy and forgiveness, or do you tend to gloss over it as no big deal?

4. While some of us are flippant about our sin, others of us allow the weight of it to crush us. We attach ourselves to our failures and carry them around. Anytime we do something good we hear the voice of condemnation whispering in the background, "Remember what you did. You are a fake. You can never be truly good." Without realizing it, we act as if we know better than God by refusing to forgive ourselves for what He has already forgiven. Is there anything that happened in your past friendships for which you are unable to forgive yourself? How has your refusal to accept forgiveness become a burden in your life?

Even if we know God forgives us and we are able to forgive ourselves, forgiving others is a different story. It is natural for us to make excuses for our own bad behavior while condemning the bad behavior of others. When injustice is committed against us, we crave justice deeply.

5. Read Matthew 18:28–35. What did the servant do after he had been forgiven? How much did the other servant owe him?

The king forgave the first servant for an unfathomable sum owed, but the servant's peer owed him only one hundred days wages. Even in light of the king's mercy, the servant couldn't forgive his peer. It can be so hard to forgive those who have wronged us. It feels horrible to find out that we have been the subject of gossip, are the object of betrayal, or that we weren't worth the hard conversation that would have kept a friendship alive.

Those wrongs are real. They hurt us. They create fresh wounds in our hearts or dig deeper into the ones that are already there. Our feelings are valid and true. But in light of eternity, these offenses do not even come close to the way that each of us have offended God. If we have been forgiven for our massive, unpayable debt against God, He commands that we forgive lesser debts.

We must respond to His command. Will it feel good to let the wrongs go? Maybe not at first, but God honors an obedient heart. He will bring about the freedom He has promised.

How do we actually put into action the practice of forgiveness? We start by specifically naming the thing that needs to be forgiven. In the parable above, we know exactly how much money each servant owed to his debtor. It was that amount and only that amount that could be forgiven. Once we have named the debt, we release the other person from the debt that they owe. We don't have to say that whatever happened is "ok." It may not be. Instead, we name the thing for which we are forgiving. In doing so, we declare the other person free from whatever it is that we think they owe us. We hand the power of justice to God and free ourselves from whatever happened.

6. Is there a situation in your life in which you are finding it hard to forgive? How were you hurt? Be specific. Name the debt. What do you think that you are owed? Can you let go of the debt and let God be the dealer of justice?

Quiet your heart and enjoy His presence. . . Forgiveness restores us, body and soul.

The difference between someone who is free and someone who is imprisoned is a stark one. The free person can go wherever they please. They are free to eat good food, spend time outside, engage in relationships with loved ones, and appreciate the beauty of nature. A prisoner eats what is given, rarely spends time outside, barely talks to loved ones, and is unable to experience anything beyond the walls of the prison.

When we choose to hold on to grudges, no matter how right we may be, we are our own jailers. We build the walls that keep us from all that God offers us. It is impossible to have healthy relationships if we are constantly keeping track of what everyone owes us. Grudges keep us from seeing others how God sees them. We are so busy maximizing their faults that we can't see that God has forgiven our debtors as well. Grace requires more.

When we forgive, the weight is lifted. Choosing forgiveness frees us from attachments to specific transgressions. It frees us from defining ourselves, someone else, or a relationship according to one bad act. Studies have shown that when we forgive, we sleep better, our blood pressure is lower, and we deal with less anxiety and depression. When we let go of the spiritual weight, we reap the benefits in our physical health. It is worth it to forgive.

When Christ forgave us, He set us free from the burden of sin. Why would we willingly place ourselves in chains that have already been broken? Yes, friendships deal out wounds, but God's grace and mercy outweigh everything. Where do you need healing in your friendships? Start with forgiveness. It is a process and it may take you a while to forgive completely but take the first step. God honors your obedience and He will walk with you through the process and into freedom.

"Be kind to one another, tenderhearted, forgiving one another, as God in Christ forgave you."
(Ephesians 4:32)

Conclusion

According to Nehemiah 6, it took the Israelites fifty-two days to completely rebuild the wall. Jerusalem's enemies were discouraged because they knew that the work had only been finished with God's help. Nehemiah wisely set up guards to foster the protection provided by the wall and then turned his attention inward to the nation of Israel. It was time to celebrate. Nehemiah and Ezra, another important religious leader, called the people together for a large festival. Over weeks, they read the Jewish law, celebrated the ancient Feast of Tabernacles, made a public confession of sins, and vowed to live their lives according to God's covenant.

Now that the wall was in place, the people of God had the protection they needed to become a thriving nation. They had the freedom to pursue God without fear of outside forces. The opportunity for total restoration was on the horizon.

Unfortunately, the story of Nehemiah does not end with the people of Jerusalem becoming the people of glory that God desired. Having done the work to fortify their city, they neglected to allow God to transform them from the inside as well as the outside. Following the festival, Nehemiah inspected the city again. He found that the temple was being neglected and the people had failed to hold up their vow to live according to God's law. They had protected themselves from outside invaders but they had not worked on their own hearts.[26]

Dear sister, we must do the work to heal from past hurts in our friendships. We must put the guardrails into place to recognize toxic friendships and set up appropriate personal boundaries. In the end, He doesn't want to simply build around us a wall of protection. He wants to transform us. He desires that we radiate with His love so we become the kind of women that bring the health and love of Christ into every single relationship, especially our friendships.

In Jesus Christ, you become a new creation. You are no longer a woman with a wall around a heart of darkness. You became a woman who has been transformed from the inside out. Your boundaries are informed by Christ-like maturity, not fear of hurt and failure. God has given you a heart of flesh where there was once a heart of stone (Ezekiel 36:26). He can do it all. He can protect you from outside hurts and heal you from your inside sins. When He is done, your relationships will be transformed because **you** have been transformed.

Want to learn more about this week's topic? Don't miss Lesson 4's short video from Mallory at walkingwithpurpose.com/videos.

My Resolution

In what specific way will I apply what I learned in this lesson?

Example:

1. I will perform an examination of conscience at the end of every day and ask myself, "Who is the point?" If I have placed myself in the center of my universe, I will ask God to give me the grace to recognize that He is the point and that I am a player in His story. I will then write down how I have placed myself at the center, examine whether or not I am experiencing freedom or making up stories, and write down the reality of what is happening regardless of my own take on things.

2. If I am experiencing a toxic friendship, I will bring the concentric circle exercise to prayer and ask the Lord what role this friendship has in my life. If I need advice, I will seek the wise counsel of a spiritual director or priest for ideas on how to move forward with this friendship.

3. I will sit in adoration and make a list of personal boundaries that I need to place in my relationships. I will then ask a close friend to help me implement them in my relationships and hold me accountable.

My Resolution:

Catechism Clips of the Catholic Church

CCC 1872 Sin is an act contrary to reason. It wounds man's nature and injures human solidarity.

NOTES

NOTES

NOTES

Lesson 5

BECOMING A GREAT FRIEND

Introduction

Years ago, I heard a teacher talk about the difference between gifting and character. Defining his terms, he told us that our giftings are the natural abilities that God has given to each of us. These are things like being good at sports or academics without having to put in much effort. We may have a knack for hospitality, thrive in administrative work, or excel in public speaking.

He then explained that our character is our ability to live a moral life. It is made up of things like our level of honesty, integrity, or work ethic. Our character determines our ability to act honorably when faced with a conflict. "While our world values gifting over character," he said, "How we develop our character will always be more important than our gifting."

We can see proof of the importance of character throughout the Old Testament. God repeatedly poured out blessing upon blessing over the Israelites. He gifted them internally by setting them apart as His chosen people. Externally, He showered them with miracles and saved them from their enemies. In spite of all of this, too many of the individual Israelites failed to display good character at critical times in their lives. They wanted God on their side, but all too often, did not live in obedience to His will. What did they need in order to handle the responsibilities that came with the blessing of being His chosen people? They needed character.

In fairness to the Israelites, they did not have the gift of the indwelling Holy Spirit. But we do. This should be a game changer for us. God has given us everything we need to obey Him. We've got internal and external gifts from Him, and most importantly, the Holy Spirit is continuously offering us the strength to do the hard thing. But if we fail to allow Him to mold and build our character, we will be unequipped to live how He asks us to live. We will neglect our gifts, and we will miss out on the fullness of the joy that He offers.

God can bless us with good friends. He can get us out of bad situations and heal us from past wounds. But without a transformation of the heart, we will continue to get into the same messes and respond to conflict in the same ways. If we refuse to lay down our modern idols and give ourselves to God, our friendships will always fall short of what God has planned for them.

This transformation is exactly what we will explore in this lesson. How do we become women whose lives resemble Christ's life? How do we become capable of enjoying excellent relationships with other women?

How do we begin? By giving Him one "yes" at a time. We choose God over everything else. We choose Him and His ways over other philosophies and practices. Then, He slowly transforms us into women who have the Christ-like integrity to develop mature, God-centered friendships. With our eyes on Jesus, we become women who are more focused on others than on self. Our friendships will have the potential to reach the heights of divine joy and goodness.

No matter where you are today, dear sister, know that God walks with **you**. He knows that holiness is a process and will do the work required if you let Him.

"The Lord judges the peoples; judge me, O Lord, according to my righteousness and according to the integrity that is in me." (Psalm 7:8)

Day One
FALLING IN LOVE WITH THE GOOD

We have spent the previous lessons of this study discovering God's purpose for friendship, the behaviors that get in the way of His purpose, and how to heal from the dysfunction that we've dealt to others and felt ourselves. Now, it's time for us to look inside ourselves and ask, what are we bringing to the table? Are we the type of women with whom other women should want to spend time? Or do we carry drama and strife into our friendships? If this question makes you jump to all of your imperfections, fear not. Philippians 1:6 reminds us that "he who started a good work among you will bring it to completion." Each of us is a work in progress, but God will continue to conform our hearts to His if we let Him.

1. Read Mark 5:25–34.

    A. What was the woman's issue and how did she try to address it in verses 25 and 26? Did it work?

    B. How was this woman finally healed of her bleeding, according to verses 27–30?

    C. What did Jesus say to her once He realized that she had touched Him and been healed?

Imagine for a moment what it must have been like for this woman to be dealing with hemorrhages for twelve long years. Even if she was able to clean herself up on the outside and hide the bleeding from others, her condition plagued every moment. There was a wound inside of her that affected her entire being whether others saw it or not. It was only when she, with a heart full of faith, reached out to Jesus that she experienced complete transformation. When she touched Him, her hemorrhaging disappeared, and she became a new creation. Jesus then told her to live the life of a woman who had been healed inside and out, a woman completely transformed and at peace.

2. In the same way that hemorrhaging was an internal issue for the woman, sin is an internal issue for us. What God did for the woman, He also did for us to a greater and more glorious degree. According to Ephesians 2:1–10, how did God heal us through Jesus, and what does that mean for our lives?

3. Take a moment to reflect on what God has done in your life. Write a specific example of how the Lord brought you from death to life. What transformation took place and how are you living differently now?

4. If God brought us from death to life, then how are we supposed to respond according to Colossians 3:1–3?

5. There is a major difference between focusing on following God's rules and setting our hearts on the things that are above. Read Galatians 5:17–25 and answer the following questions in order to better understand the difference.

A. What are some sinful actions (works of the flesh) according to Saint Paul? See Galatians 5:19-21.

Those are the things we are to avoid. But is it enough to just follow God's rules and omit these things from your life? Saint Paul goes on to show that something more is needed.

B. What are the fruits of the Spirit? See Galatians 5:22-23.

C. How does Saint Paul tell us to live? See Galatians 5:25.

Jesus, through the sacrifice of Himself, calls us to move beyond following the rules. He invites us into a living relationship with God in which we continually become more like Him. We should increasingly display the fruits of the Spirit in the way we treat people.

But all too often, our lives only look different from the rest of the lives in the world because we have added an extra check list of religious "to do's" to our lives. We go to Mass on Sunday and then easily engage in gossip or mean-spirited treatment of other women. We spend a bit of time reciting the rosary before we give hours to a Netflix show that damages hearts and minds. We waste time scrolling through the lives of other people while ignoring the good that can be done in our own lives and community. We preach good values to our children while giving into our own secret sexual temptations. If we are to become true women of God, we must go beyond lip service to the rules. We must allow Him to change our hearts.

So how do we do it? First, we need to recognize that the more we love God, the more we will love what He loves. Our heart starts to align with His. From there, He can take us further down the path to holiness. The more time we spend with Him, talk to Him, learn about Him, and obey Him, the more we will love Him and *want* to obey Him. Second, we need to recognize that His desires have a higher priority than our desires. When our desires don't match what God desires, we choose to do what God desires anyway. When we fail, we run to the Father through the sacrament of Reconciliation and begin again.

6. Think about your relationship with God. Be honest. Are you genuinely seeking to love what He loves? Or do you follow the rules while giving your heart to things of the world? Take a moment to reflect on where you really are right now. What step could you take to genuinely become a lover of the good?

Quiet your heart and enjoy His presence… He wants to surprise the world through your goodness.

The story of Ebenezer Scrooge in A Christmas Carol *is one with which most of us are familiar. A greedy, old miser, Scrooge, is the meanest man in his town. Naturally, his least favorite holiday is Christmas. One Christmas, Scrooge's old business partner, Jacob Marley, visits him from the afterlife to warn him to change his ways. Scrooge is then visited by the ghosts of Christmas past, present and future, who teach him lessons that change his heart.*

The story ends joyfully. Scrooge experiences a conversion of heart and becomes a new man, one who can keep Christmas well. At the end of the book, Dickens describes the new Ebenezer Scrooge. "Scrooge was better than his word. He did it all, and infinitely more…He became as good a friend, as good a master, and as good a man as the good old city knew, or any other good old city, town, or borough in the good old world."[27]

Our world no longer believes that people can be as good as they seem. We have become so cynical. A tidal wave of scandals, lies, and secrets has left us suspicious of anyone who seems to be genuinely good

---

27 Charles Dickens, *A Christmas Carol* (England: Wordsworth Editions Limited, 1995), 79.

or genuinely holy. We are constantly waiting for skeletons to jump out of the closets, and unfortunately, they often do.

What if you were different? What if you softened the hearts of your friends by living your life as a woman of fierce integrity? What if you were exactly who you are in public and in private? What if you surprised our broken society by becoming the woman who was better than her word, the type of woman who elevated every conversation and who brought the light of Christ to every relationship?

Rules tell us just how close to the edge we can get before we cross a line. Life in the Spirit, however, launches us into an endless sky because God's goodness is an infinite aspiration. Only He can get us there, but He is constantly waiting for us to give Him permission to renew our hearts. Take a deep breath and let Him transform you. Leave behind anything that you love that God doesn't. Live as a woman who has been healed from the inside out.

Day Two
BECOMING A WOMAN OF WISDOM

Every woman embodies some of God's goodness. Some women are kind, funny, or generous, while others are thoughtful or genuine. All of these are wonderful qualities that will bless any friendship, but there is something remarkable about a woman of true wisdom. While most women offer one another advice based on the conventional wisdom of the world, a truly wise woman offers Godly, eternal wisdom to her friends. Her presence, her perspective, and her counsel challenge other women to make better decisions and rise to a higher standard of character. Scripture tells us that this type of wisdom is only given by God. It is a precious gift, and He offers it to us all.

1. Read Proverbs 3:13–18.

   List below all of the ways that wisdom is described in this passage.

The writer of Proverbs says wisdom is better than everything we desire. Wisdom sounds like something we should all be chasing after with abandon, but what exactly is it? Without a proper definition of wisdom, we confuse it with knowledge or intelligence. Knowledge is information gathered about certain subjects. Intelligence is the ability to gather that information. Saint Thomas Aquinas defined wisdom for us in the following way: "Wisdom is both knowledge of and judgement about 'divine things' and the ability to judge and direct human affairs according to divine truth."[28] In layman's terms, wisdom is the ability to see our situations from God's perspective and apply His will to our particular circumstances. While wise people may also have knowledge and intelligence, not all knowledgeable and intelligent people have wisdom.

2. Over and over again, Scripture compares the wise to the foolish in practical, everyday situations. How do the following verses distinguish the actions of a wise person from the actions of a foolish person?

    Proverbs 13:16

    Proverbs 12:15

    Proverbs 10:14

    Notice the contrast between how the wise and the foolish make decisions. The wise act with prudence and humility. They seek counsel and study before making major decisions. The foolish react immediately and indulge their feelings. They are too proud to seek counsel or outside knowledge before making decisions.

3. How do you make decisions and react to situations? Are you quick to anger, always saying exactly what is on your mind without apology? Do you seek to get even with others while failing to consider the consequences? Do you make choices based solely on your own preferences? Or are you slow to speak, gathering all the information and considering God's purpose in your response? Are you prudent in your decision making, thinking of the long-term consequences with others' preferences in mind? Would you consider yourself a woman who acts out of God's wisdom? Why or why not?

---

28 Saint Thomas Aquina, "Summa Theologica," New Advent, 1/21/2020, https://www.newadvent.org/summa/3045.htm.

4. The Lord has given us all the direction we need to leave behind our foolish ways. How does the Bible say that we can gain wisdom?

    A. What is the beginning of wisdom according to Psalm 111:10?

The Hebrew word for "fear" is "yarah," which means honor, respect, reverence, and worshipful awe.[29] To fear God means so much more than being frightened of Him. When we come face to face with the reality of His glory, power, and might against our smallness, we fear Him. That is, we take God seriously.

    B. Where should we place our trust according to Proverbs 3:5? Should we rely on our own understanding?

    C. What does James 1:5 say we should do if we are lacking wisdom?

Is it possible that so many Christians are not wise because we don't take Him seriously, rely on Him, or ask Him for wisdom? We tend to see God as a product of our invention. He is there to make us happy and tell us that everything will be ok. He agrees with us more than He disagrees with us. We see Jesus as a friend of sinners and forget that in love, He commands sinners to go and sin no more. When we make God in our image, God's perspective looks eerily like our perspective. We seem wise in our own eyes even when we are actually fools. True wisdom begins with seeing God for who He is, taking God at His word, and conforming ourselves to His ways instead of trying to get Him to conform to ours.

5. Who embodies all wisdom according to Colossians 2:2–3?

Jesus said that if we have seen Him, we have seen the Father (John 14:9). All of the wisdom and understanding available to us can be found in Christ. In Him we gain the treasures of wisdom that are more precious than gold; we find the everyday path that will lead to peace. He is the source of a profound change that begins in

---

29 Lois Tverbert, "Yarah-Fear of the Lord," Engedi Resource Center, 06/30/2015, https://engediresourcecenter. com/2015/06/30/yarah-fear-of-the-lord/.

us, extends through us, and then touches the world. The more time we spend with Him, and the more we do what He says, the wiser we will become.

6. Reflect on your own relationship with Jesus, no matter where you are with Him. How will spending even a little bit more time with Him, studying Him, and following His word change how you see the world and how you make decisions?

Quiet your heart and enjoy His presence… Jesus is the firm foundation.

Everyone then who hears these words of mine and does them will be like a wise man who built his house upon the rock; and the rain fell, and the floods came, and the winds blew and beat upon that house, but it did not fall, because it had been founded on the rock. And everyone who hears these words of mine and does not do them will be like a foolish man who built his house upon the sand; and the rain fell, and the floods came, and the winds blew and beat against that house, and it fell, and great was the fall of it. (Matthew 7:24–28)

Your potential for wisdom depends upon your foundation. In this passage from Matthew's gospel, Jesus uses the imagery of the house built on the rock and the house built on sand. The house built on sand fell while the house built on rock stood firm. The foundation of the house built on sand was ever shifting, changing with the weather. Every time the house moved; the foundation moved. It couldn't hold the house up against the storms of the world. The foundation of the second house was much different. It was one, solid, immovable rock. Because it was so strong, it didn't matter how the storms of the world railed against the house. Yes, the house may have been harmed by its circumstances, but it didn't fall. The foundation stood firm.

What is your foundation? Is it the ever-changing values of society, or is it Jesus Christ who is the same yesterday, today, and tomorrow (Hebrews 13:8)? So many women in our world are buffeted and blown around by events in their lives. What if they looked at you and saw a woman who was unshakable? You can be the woman who walks with an eternal perspective and offers the wisdom of God.

Day Three
BECOMING A WOMAN OF VIRTUE

If you want to be a good friend, start by becoming a woman who is continually conforming herself to the image of God. The more that order and peace reigns in your inner life, the more order and peace you naturally bring into your friendships. On Day One and Day Two of this lesson, we explored how we can become wise women who love what is good. Loving what God loves and seeing what God sees only makes a difference if it changes our behavior. We must not only love good, but we must also *do* good. We must not only see the world from God's perspective, but we must *act* in accord with that perspective. When we do act in accordance with God's perspective, we live a life of virtue. According to the ancient philosophers and saints, a virtuous life is the avenue to living "the good life," and only virtuous persons attain genuinely virtuous friendships.

1. How does the Bible tell us that we are to live in manner and conduct?

    A. Of what should our lives be worthy? See Philippians 1:27.

    B. According to 1 Peter 1:15–16, how should we be in our conduct?

    C. How does James 1:23–25 contrast the difference between someone who hears God's word and applies it to his life versus someone who hears God's word and does not apply it to his life?

    D. Virtue is more than making the right decision once or twice, it's a way of life. How does the *Catechism of the Catholic Church* define virtue? What is the goal of a virtuous life? See CCC 1803.

In *True Friendship,* Dr. John Cuddeback gives insight into how we should live.

The key questions about a human person's way of life are: Does the person understand what is truly most important, and does the person live in a way that reflects this understanding? To live as though what is most important really is most important is to live an ordered life, a good life, a happy life. To live as though inferior things are most important is to live a disordered life, a bad life, an unhappy life.[30]

2. The belief that there is no such thing as absolute truth is a popular one these days. This belief gets in the way of the pursuit of the good life, because it becomes impossible to define what is inherently good. Pope Emeritus Benedict XVI warned of the dangers of this belief, saying, "We are moving toward a dictatorship of relativism which does not recognize anything as for certain and which has as its highest goal one's own ego and one's own desires."[31] Our modern culture breathes relativism—the idea that the definition of right and wrong, good and bad, can shift in relation to culture, society, or historical context. But as Benjamin D. Wiker wrote, "Relativism is a poison. It attacks our most human capacity, the capacity to seek and know the truth."[32]

    Have you experienced the consequences of living as though there is no such thing as right and wrong? Have you ever observed someone (perhaps yourself) shifting the definition of right and wrong in order to suit one's ego or desires? Can you see how relativism can dampen the desire to seek and know the truth? Write about what you've experienced.

It only takes a quick search online to find an infinite amount of research and opinions on how to live. With all of the noise, it can be difficult to discern exactly how to live a life of virtue. When we find ourselves faced with millions of modern opinions, it is a good rule of thumb to consider ancient wisdom first. Jeremiah 6:16 says, "Stand by the roads, and look, and ask for the ancient paths, where the good way is; and walk in it, and find rest for your souls." The church not only tells us that there is a right way to live, but she also reveals to us *what* it is and *how* to do it.

---

30 John Cuddeback, *True Friendship: Where Virtue Becomes Happiness* (Epic Publishing: Denver, 2010), 5.

31 Benjamin D. Wiker, "Benedict vs. the Great Dictatorship of Relativism," February 25, 2013, *National Catholic Register*, https://www.ncregister.com/blog/benedict-vs-the-dictatorship-of-relativism.

32 Ibid.

3. The church condenses all of the attributes of righteous living into four cardinal virtues. From these virtues, all other human virtues flow. Define each according to the Catechism.

    Prudence (see CCC 1806)

    Justice (see CCC 1807)

    Fortitude (see CCC 1808)

    Temperance (see CCC 1809)

When we resist overindulging in life's pleasures by saying no to one more sweet, one more drink, or one more swipe of the credit card, we practice temperance. When we commit to God and trust in His plan, regardless of misfortunes and bad circumstances, we practice fortitude. When we speak up or stay silent, act or refrain from acting based on obedience to God and the good of His people, we practice prudence. And when we offer to God all that He deserves—our worship, our time, our money, our talents—and we treat every neighbor with dignity and respect, we practice justice.

Living and practicing these cardinal virtues will lead to a well-lived life, a happy life. These virtues lead to flourishing in our friendships. If we are able to practice prudence, justice, fortitude and temperance, we will direct our friendship towards the good. If we are living a good and happy life, we will want the very same things for those we love. Our friendships will naturally be directed toward the greatest good.

If you want to live a virtuous life, you must fight for it daily. Most of us know what is important, but we don't live what we know. We know that love of God is most important, but we allow ourselves to be ruled by our passions. We know that integrity is important, but we don't have the strength to hold onto ours when a slightly immoral opportunity presents itself. The virtuous life is the best life, but it is one that is hard to build.

4. If you find yourself struggling to put your love of God into action, take heart. The saints struggled with this very same thing.

   A. How does Saint Paul describe his struggle to live a holy life in Romans 7:14–15?

   B. Why is living the virtuous life so hard for us to attain according to CCC 1810 and 1811? What helps us to live that virtue and what part is our responsibility?

5. What is it in your life that is keeping you from living a life of virtue? Why is this thing such an obstacle in your life? Take a moment to explore this. Then, write out a prayer to God specifically asking Him for His grace. Ask Him to build in you the character to do the good that you struggle to achieve.

Quiet your heart and enjoy His presence… He is leading you to love.

"And now these three remain: faith, hope and love. But the greatest of these is love." (1 Corinthians 13:13)

Read the following verses that describe love. You have heard each of these lines before. This time, as you go through, cross out each instance of the word "love" and "it" and write in your own name.

> *Love is patient, love is kind. It does not envy, it does not boast, it is not proud. It does not dishonor others, it is not self-seeking, it is not easily angered, it keeps no record of wrongs. Love does not delight in evil but rejoices with the truth. It always protects, always trusts, always hopes, always perseveres. Love never fails. (1 Corinthians 13: 4–8)*

Does the verse still ring true? Which pieces do not? Offer this verse with your name in it as a prayer to our Lord. Thank Him for the ways that He has built His ways into the very core of your being. Ask Him to build virtue where you are lacking.

Day Four
LOVING WITH THE LOVE OF CHRIST

In the "Quiet Your Heart" section of the last lesson, you went through 1 Corinthians 13:4–8 and wrote your name over the word "love." Were you surprised with how many attributes of love weren't quite congruent with your name? If you were, don't be discouraged. When Jesus told His disciples to "Love one another, as I have loved you" (John 15:12), He knew that He was asking the impossible. The truth is that it is not in our fallen nature to love as Christ loves. Our love is limited by selfishness. On our own terms, love will always fall short and eventually become self-serving. Still, Jesus commanded us to love others with a love that is higher than our grasp because He is the one who can lift us up to reach His love. Only through this type of love can we experience the fullness of God's joy and goodness in our friendships.

1. Let's look into the Old Testament for a glimpse of how justice was handled before Christ came.

    A. Read Exodus 21:23–25. Write out what it says to do.

    B. Read Leviticus 24:19–20. What instructions are given here?

    C. Was this approach to justice based on self-sacrificing love or fairness?

The attitude of the ancient world, and most of human history, was "might makes right" and "he who has the power makes the rules." Even the Hebrew law of "eye for eye, tooth for tooth" (Exodus 21:24) was an attempt to promote fairness and curb the brutality of revenge. History proves that when we're left to our own devices, we want to dominate and control each other.

Can you see any remnants of this attitude in our modern culture? Even though our world may seem a bit kinder and more equitable than cultures of the past, the more we move away from God, the more the "might makes right" mentality rears its ugly head.

Consider how we treat each other when it comes to opinions and politics. Our culture says there is no longer a universal definition of right and wrong when it comes to living the moral life. So all too often, we base our judgement of others on their opinions and political affiliations. And if we don't like who they vote for, we don't like them. We tear others apart without ever trying to understand their point of view or having the humility to seek truth on moral issues from God's perspective. In a society where moral truth is no longer defined by God, people treasure their self-defined truths. Even though these truths are actually opinions, we use them as our metrics for "good people" and "bad people." While we may think that we have become a kinder society, the truth is that "might makes right" remains alive and well. Our only hope, our only way back, is through Jesus, the Way, the Truth, and the Life.

2. How did Jesus address the Jewish law of "an eye for an eye" in Matthew 5:38–42? What new directions did He give?

3. How does this teaching make you feel? Do you find it easy to act toward others in love, to go that extra mile, even when it doesn't feel fair? Why or why not?

If this teaching makes you uncomfortable, it's because "turning the other cheek" and "going the extra mile" feels weak. Most of us are much more at home in a world of fairness where people get what they deserve. Although it may feel more natural to want to get even or treat our friends how they treat us, this type of behavior typically leads to drama and hurt feelings. Jesus showed us that selfless love leads to better relationships.

4. Jesus lived out radical love in all of His interactions. Read John 4:7–39 and recount the story below highlighting the way that Jesus treated the woman in the story. How did He speak to her? What did He say and how did He say it? How did He show her love and what was the end result?

This exchange between Jesus and the Samaritan woman reveals four characteristics of the way Jesus loved.

Jesus' love was **self-sacrificial**. In this story, it was against societal norms for a Jew to spend time with a Samaritan or for a man to have that kind of conversation with a woman. Jesus did not care about societal norms. He saw a woman who was loved by God and was willing to sacrifice His reputation to speak with her.

Jesus' love was **humble**. Jesus met this woman in her humanity. He did not expect her to be more than she was but instead simply spoke to her about what was going on in her life at that moment. That being said, Jesus did not leave her in her mess— He offered her another way.

His love was **grounded in Truth**. He understood where she was coming from and why she made the choices that she made, but He did not waver between right and wrong. He kindly challenged her to find the Truth.

Finally, Jesus' love was **divine**. His love reached beyond human nature and led people to the deepest desires of their human hearts: God. The Samaritan woman walked away unashamed because through the love of Jesus, she encountered the living God.

5. If we want to love others as Jesus loved us, we should take on the same characteristics: self-sacrificial, humble, grounded in Truth, and divine. We will only exhibit these if we allow Jesus to work in and through us. The good news? He is already working. Next to the four attributes below, write one way that you love others well and one way that you can get better. Ask God to give you what you need to love in this way.

Self-Sacrificial

Humble

Grounded in Truth

Divine

Quiet your heart and enjoy His presence… His love for you goes further than you can imagine.

Jesus offers His love for you in the exact same way that He offered it to the woman at the well. He meets you exactly where you are. Not only does He understand the details of your life and the choices that you make, He went so far as to become a human being Himself to do so. The Word of God, in the most selfless act of all time, descended to earth and entered into humanity in the form of a baby. He lived the life of a poor traveler, was crucified, died, was buried, and rose again, all with you in mind. In His love for you, He laid Himself down completely. Can you do the same for others? If you can't, He can. Let Him do it through you.

His love for you is humble. He offers His entire self to you in the Eucharist—body, blood, soul, and divinity—just so He could become one with you every time you receive Communion. Can you humble yourself for others? If you can't, He can. Let Him do it through you.

His love for you is grounded in Truth. He meets you where you are, but His love is not mere empathy. It leads somewhere. He walks with you—not behind you, and not ahead of you—to lead you to the Truth that will set you free. Can you love people in Truth? If you can't, He can. Let Him do it through you.

His love for you is divine. His love goes beyond human nature; it's a love that makes you whole, and brings you to your heart's desire, the God of the universe. Can you love others in such a way that they see and want God? If you can't, He can. Let Him do it through you.

Maybe you think this is too much to ask. Most who heard Jesus say, "Be perfect, as your heavenly Father is perfect" (Matthew 5:48) thought the statement was outrageous. But our God is the God of miracles, and He didn't leave us alone. He left us the Holy Spirit, the ever-present spirit of Truth. Call on Him and let Him love others through you. Your love will go so much further than you thought it could.

Pray this prayer of Saint Francis. Sit with the words and allow them to take hold in your heart.

> *Lord, make me an instrument of your peace*
> *Where there is hatred, let me sow love*
> *Where there is injury, pardon*
> *Where there is doubt, faith*
> *Where there is despair, hope*
> *Where there is darkness, light*
> *And where there is sadness, joy*
>
> *O Divine Master, grant that I may*
> *Not so much seek to be consoled as to console*
> *To be understood, as to understand*

To be loved, as to love
For it is in giving that we receive
And it's in pardoning that we are pardoned
And it's in dying that we are born to Eternal Life

Amen

Day Five
BEING WILLING TO GO FIRST

A key attribute of a great friend is that she is willing to go first. She is willing to make the call, send the text, offer help, or initiate a gathering. Not many women live this way. The more common scenario is that women miss out on building friendships—good intentions and good ideas go unacted upon. Saint John reminds us in 1 John 4:19 that, "We love because He *first* loved us," (emphasis added). God is the initiator and inviter in His relationship with us. He pursues us with a relentless love, and we must be willing to do the same for others.

1. In Luke 7:36–50, Jesus sat at the house of a Pharisee to dine. A sinful woman learned of Jesus' presence and went to Him with an alabaster flask of ointment. The woman proceeded to wet Jesus' feet with her tears, wipe them with her hair, kiss His feet, and anoint Him with oil. The Pharisee, offended by the act, admonished Jesus for allowing the woman to bless Him in this way.

    A. Read Luke 7:44–47. How does Jesus respond to the Pharisee? How does He distinguish the woman's actions from the Pharisee's actions?

    B. Read Luke 4:37–38 and write down three things that stand out to you about how this woman acted toward Jesus.

The most striking thing about this woman is her audacity. She did not wait to be invited. Instead, she saw an opportunity to initiate love and took action. She perceived a need in her Lord, and she met that need with extravagance (anointing Him with the best oil) and abandonment (unphased by what others might think).

Have you ever noticed the relief that comes upon a woman's face when someone finally offers her the help that she needs? Have you seen the expression on her face when she is invited to something for which her weary heart is longing? Why is it, then, that we so often let good intentions toward each other go unfulfilled? We allow our fears of rejection and our wounds from the past keep us from taking action. The Lord prompts us to act—whether it's offering help to a woman who needs it, inviting a new friend to go on a walk, or offering to walk with an old friend through a new problem—but so often, we just say no.

2. Can you remember a time that you felt prompted to reach out to another woman with the hand of help and friendship but didn't? What kept you from turning your intentions into actions?

3. What insight does Saint John give us into the relationship between love and fear in 1 John 4:18?

We know from experience that reaching out to others requires courage and vulnerability. Sometimes we will be embarrassed and rejected. Our fears will be realized and we may receive new wounds, but rejection is the cost of true love. Jesus was rejected by the world that He loved. Under His crown of glory lie the scars of the love that He poured out for us. He told us that we will experience much of what He experienced. Waiting to feel completely safe before reaching out, will cause us to miss out on the joy that comes through risk.

Initiating an act of love does not mean imposing ourselves on others with no consideration for what they actually need or want. But we should act when the Holy Spirit moves us. When we think that we should pick up the phone or extend the invitation, we should not allow fear to tell us no or give into the lure of self-preservation. Mel Robbins, speaker, television host, and author, explained in her Ted Talk that if we don't marry a good intention with an action within the first five seconds that we feel a spark of inspiration, we will kill the inspiration and most likely never follow through.[33] We can follow through and initiate love with the same tenacity, extravagance, and abandon as the woman who anointed Jesus' feet.

---

33 Mel Robbins, "How to Stop Screwing Yourself Over," TEDx Talks, YouTube Video, 21:39. 06/11/2011, https://www.ted.com/talks/mel_robbins_how_to_stop_screwing_yourself_over?language=en.

4. The Lord knows that our acts of love may go unnoticed or not be reciprocated. He knows the risk that we take when we decide to be the initiator. Yet, what does Jesus tell us in Luke 6:38?

Regardless of how our acts of love are received, God sees all. He knows our hearts and intentions. He knows the courage it takes to reach out, and He is delighted when we love like He loves. He will ultimately respond with kindness and generosity.

5. Is God asking you to reach out to someone in friendship? Maybe you have reached out before but have not been able to connect. Maybe you have lost touch and need to pick up the phone. Maybe there is a woman in your community who has been on your heart even though she is outside of your circle. Who is she, and what is the Lord asking you to do? Will you do it?

Quiet your heart and enjoy His presence… He has made you to be a light to the world.

You are the light of the world. A town built on a hill cannot be hidden. Neither do people light a lamp and put it under a bowl. Instead they put it on its stand, and it gives light to everyone in the house. In the same way, let your light shine before others, that they may see your good deeds and glorify your Father in heaven. (Matthew 5:14–16)

'You are the sum of the five people you spend the most time with.' You've probably heard that one before now. But what if one friend is somehow different than the others? Let me tell you what I experienced when I met Andrea. I had left my faith behind years before I started working with her. The first day that we worked together, we clicked, but there was something about Andrea that bothered me. I found myself annoyed with her when she had been nothing but nice. I thought about it for a few days and realized that I was annoyed by Andrea's joy. She was just too joyful, and I couldn't figure out why.

Andrea started inviting me to do things outside of work. Before long, we were going on walks, eating dinners together, and I was even attending her church. Andrea continued to invite me into friendship and I began to respond. Over time, I realized that the joy that I had found so annoying at the beginning of our friendship was the joy of Jesus Christ, Andrea's first love. Eventually, all of Andrea's invitations led me to give my life to Jesus. Because of one woman who decided to pursue a friendship with me, my life was completely changed.

Dear sister, when Jesus said in Matthew 5:14 that "You are the light of the world," He meant you! When you say yes to Him, you shine His goodness into this dark world. Other women are changed, maybe forever, when they see the light of the One who is in you. Please don't hide the light, it's too important. We must initiate, because our world is lonely and we are interacting with each other only if we can keep part of ourselves hidden. Many people no longer believe in true love or true friendship. Cynicism overshadows the possibility of a true God. Let your light shine before others, so that when women meet you, they want the joy that you have and are led to its true source.

Conclusion

In 12th century Assisi, Italy, a young woman named Clare heard a local preacher, Francis, teach during a Lenten service. Already a woman of deep prayer, she was attracted to Francis's message of living out the Gospel radically through poverty, prayer, and service to the poor. She approached him and asked him to teach her to live out the Gospel, and a friendship was born. Their friendship launched a new order of religious life for men and women who wanted to give their lives to Jesus and His Church in a radical way. Today, the Franciscans and the Poor Clares are still alive and well, serving all over the world. Shortly after their deaths, both of these remarkable people were canonized saints. The fruit of their friendship is still evident in the world today.[34]

In 19th century France, a man named Louis married a woman named Zélie. Together, they had nine children, all girls, but only five survived into adulthood. Louis and Zélie were devout Catholics and immersed their daughters in the faith. All five of their daughters entered a convent. One of their daughters was Thérèse. Thérèse lived a seemingly unremarkable life and died of disease at the age of twenty-four. After her death, her writing became public and revealed the inner life of a woman so holy and so humble that Pope Pius XII commented, "She rediscovered the Gospel itself, the very heart of the Gospel."

One of the women deeply affected by her writings was her sister, Leonie. After reading Thérèse's writings, Leonie also entered religious life. Today, Louis and Zélie are both canonized saints. Thérèse became a saint so highly regarded that she is considered a "Doctor of the Church," and her sister Leonie is currently considered a Servant of God by the Church, the first step on the journey to canonized sainthood.[35] This one family, ordinary in the daily grind but extraordinary in holiness, gave us three, possibly four saints. Saint Thérèse, deeply influenced by her father's love, has brought countless men and women to Christ through her theology of the "Little Way." Her friendship with her sister may very well end in her sister's canonization.

Over the past week, we have not only laid the foundation for the character-building traits that make a great friend, but of the character traits that make great saints. Saints love God, and they love what is good. They pursue wisdom with tenacity, and they go to extraordinary lengths to love others as Christ loves. Over the centuries, the Catholic Church has held up thousands of men and women as shining examples of what it means to be a light to the world, calling a wavering world back to the unwavering faithfulness of God.

Isn't it interesting that saints tend to come in clusters and are formed through friendships? Holiness is contagious; it spreads best through friendship. These saintly relationships are the ultimate example of what it means to live out virtuous friendships that are directed toward God, and the effects echo through the centuries.

What does the Lord want to do with you? How does He want to make you holy? How does He want to change the world through your friendships? Don't miss the chance to find out. Let Him lay the foundation of your sainthood. Do the work with Him and watch Him illuminate your friendships. Your dedication to ordinary, messy, holy friendships could bring about lasting impacts in this generation and generations to come.

Want to learn more about this week's topic? Don't miss Lesson 5's short video from Mallory at walkingwithpurpose.com/videos.

My Resolution

In what specific way will I apply what I learned in this lesson?

Examples:

1. In front of the Blessed Sacrament, I will ask the Lord how He wants me to love Him more and how I can pursue wisdom in my daily life. I will journal about this topic and implement one way to pursue wisdom into my day every day.

2. I will ask a close friend of mine how I can love her better. I will humbly receive her response and then bring her answer to prayer.

3. I will think of one woman who the Holy Spirit has been bringing to my mind, and I will immediately reach out to that person with an invitation or a helping hand even if I am afraid to do it.

My Resolution:

Catechism Clips of the Catholic Church

CCC 1803 "Whatever is true, whatever is honorable, whatever is just, whatever is pure, whatever is lovely, whatever is gracious, if there is any excellence, if there is anything worthy of praise, think about these things."

A virtue is a habitual and firm disposition to do the good. It allows the person not only to perform good acts, but to give the best of himself. The virtuous person tends toward the good with all his sensory and spiritual powers; he pursues the good and chooses it in concrete actions.

The goal of a virtuous life is to become like God.

CCC 1804 Human virtues are firm attitudes, stable dispositions, habitual perfections of intellect and will that govern our actions, order our passions, and guide our conduct according to reason and faith. They make possible ease, self-mastery, and joy in leading a morally good life. The virtuous man is he who freely practices the good.

The moral virtues are acquired by human effort. They are the fruit and seed of morally good acts; they dispose of all the powers of the human being for communion with divine love.

CCC 1806 Prudence is the virtue that disposes practical reason to discern our true good in every circumstance and to choose the right means of achieving it; "the prudent man looks where he is going." "Keep sane and sober for your prayers." Prudence is "right reason in action," writes St. Thomas Aquinas, following Aristotle. It is not to be confused with timidity or fear, nor with duplicity or dissimulation. It is called auriga virtutum (the charioteer of the virtues); it guides the other virtues by setting rule and measure. It is prudence that immediately guides the judgment of conscience. The prudent man determines and directs his conduct in accordance with this judgment. With the help of this virtue we apply moral principles to particular cases without error and overcome doubts about the good to achieve and the evil to avoid.

CCC 1807 Justice is the moral virtue that consists in the constant and firm will to give their due to God and neighbor. Justice toward God is called the "virtue of religion." Justice toward men disposes one to respect the rights of each and to establish in human relationships the harmony that promotes equity with regard to persons and to the common good. The just man, often mentioned in the Sacred Scriptures, is distinguished by habitual right thinking and the uprightness of his conduct toward his neighbor. "You shall not be partial to the poor or defer to the great, but in righteousness shall you judge your neighbor." "Masters, treat your slaves justly and fairly, knowing that you also have a Master in heaven."

CCC 1808 Fortitude is the moral virtue that ensures firmness in difficulties and constancy in the pursuit of the good. It strengthens the resolve to resist temptations and to overcome obstacles in the moral life. The virtue of fortitude enables one to conquer fear, even fear of death, and to face trials and persecutions. It disposes one even to renounce and sacrifice his life in defense of a just cause. "The Lord is my strength and my song." "In the world you have tribulation; but be of good cheer, I have overcome the world."

CCC 1809 Temperance is the moral virtue that moderates the attraction of pleasures and provides balance in the use of created goods. It ensures the will's mastery over instincts and keeps desires within the limits of what is honorable. The temperate person directs the sensitive appetites toward what is good and maintains a healthy discretion: "Do not follow your inclination and strength, walking according to the desires of your heart." Temperance is often praised in the Old Testament: "Do not follow your base desires but restrain your appetites." In the New Testament it is called "moderation" or "sobriety." We ought "to live sober, upright, and godly lives in this world."

CCC 1810 Human virtues acquired by education, by deliberate acts, and by a perseverance ever-renewed in repeated efforts are purified and elevated by divine grace. With God's help, they forge character and give facility in the practice of the good. The virtuous man is happy to practice them.

CCC 1811 It is not easy for man, wounded by sin, to maintain moral balance. Christ's gift of salvation offers us the grace necessary to persevere in the pursuit of the virtues. Everyone should always ask for this grace of light and strength, frequent the sacraments, cooperate with the Holy Spirit, and follow his calls to love what is good and shun evil.

NOTES

 NOTES

Lesson 6: Connect Coffee Talk

FRIENDSHIP AND THE KINGDOM OF GOD

Accompanying talk can be viewed by DVD or digital download purchase or access online at walkingwithpurpose.com/videos.

I. **The eternal consequences of a simple friendship.**

J.R.R. Tolkien and C.S. Lewis

"The Church needs good friendships, and friendships need the Church and find their fulfillment in her." [36] –Dr. John Cuddeback, *True Friendship*

II. **Jesus started the Church through friendship.**

John 15:14–15

Matthew 28:16–20

III. **Christianity spread around the world through friendship.**

Acts 2:42

Acts 2:46-48

IV. **The impact that friendship has on society.**

A. When we decide to share life with someone, we will ultimately share with them
_____. These things, when shared between friends, will
_____.

B. "We have seen how, in friendships, persons are united in their love for one another and in their love of virtue. Friends share a vision of the good life and strive together to achieve it. Friendships thus provide 'mini communities' within the larger community; they are a basic unit, as it were, of striving for perfection. In this way the mini community of friendship is very similar to the most basic, natural unit of society, the family." [37] –Dr. John Cuddeback, *True Friendship*.

V. **The current state of friendship and society.**

VI. **How God moves through friendship.**

Saint Ignatius and Saint Francis Xavier

VII. **Do you have a vision for how your relationships affect the world around you?**

---

[37] Ibid., 76.

Questions for Discussion:

1. Is there a specific person who had a profound impact on your personal faith? If so, who were they? In what ways was that relationship a friendship?

2. Do you see evidence of the link between friendship and the state of society? How do you see them linked together? What effects do you see in society today both positive and negative? How do you think a better society would foster better friendships? What impact do you think that more virtuous friendships would have on modern society?

3. Do you often think about the way your relationships affect other people who may not be part of the relationship? Who do they affect? How do you think the Lord wants to use you and your friendships to build His kingdom on earth?

 NOTES

Appendices

 NOTES

Appendix 1
Saint Thérèse of Lisieux

Patron Saint of Walking with Purpose

Saint Thérèse of Lisieux was gifted with the ability to take the riches of our Catholic faith and explain them in a way that a child could imitate. The wisdom she gleaned from Scripture ignited a love in her heart for her Lord that was personal and transforming. The simplicity of the faith that she laid out in her writings is so completely Catholic that Pope Pius XII said, "She rediscovered the Gospel itself, the very heart of the Gospel."

Walking with Purpose is intended to be a means by which women can honestly share their spiritual struggles and embark on a journey that is refreshing to the soul. It was never intended to facilitate the deepest of intellectual study of Scripture. Instead, the focus has been to help women know Christ: to know His heart, to know His tenderness, to know His mercy, and to know His love. Our logo is a little flower, and that has meaning. When a woman begins to open her heart to God, it's like the opening of a little flower. It can easily be bruised or crushed, and it must be treated with the greatest of care. Our desire is to speak to women's hearts no matter where they are in life, baggage and all, and gently introduce truths that can change their lives.

Saint Thérèse of Lisieux, the little flower, called her doctrine "the little way of spiritual childhood," and it is based on complete and unshakable confidence in God's love for us. She was not introducing new truths. She spent countless hours reading Scripture and she shared what she found, emphasizing the importance of truths that had already been divinely revealed. We can learn so much from her:

> The good God would not inspire unattainable desires; I can, then, in spite of my littleness, aspire to sanctity. For me to become greater is impossible; I must put up with myself just as I am with all my imperfections. But I wish to find the way to go to heaven by a very straight, short, completely new little way. We are in a century of inventions: now one does not even have to take the trouble to

climb the steps of a stairway; in the homes of the rich, an elevator replaces them nicely. I, too, would like to find an elevator to lift me up to Jesus, for I am too little to climb the rough stairway of perfection. So I have looked in the books of the saints for a sign of the elevator I long for, and I have read these words proceeding from the mouth of eternal Wisdom: "He that is a little one, let him turn to me" (Proverbs 9:16). So I came, knowing that I had found what I was seeking, and wanting to know, O my God, what You would do with the little one who would answer Your call, and this is what I found:

"As one whom the mother caresses, so will I comfort you. You shall be carried at the breasts and upon the knees they shall caress you" (Isaiah 66:12–13). Never have more tender words come to make my soul rejoice. The elevator which must raise me to the heavens is Your arms, O Jesus! For that I do not need to grow; on the contrary, I must necessarily remain small, become smaller and smaller. O my God, You have surpassed what I expected, and I want to sing Your mercies. (Saint Thérèse of the Infant Jesus, *Histoire d'une Ame: Manuscrits Autobiographiques* [Paris: Éditions du Seuil, 1998], 244.)

Appendix 2
Conversion of Heart

The Catholic faith is full of beautiful traditions, rituals, and sacraments. As powerful as they are, it is possible for them to become mere habits in our lives, instead of experiences that draw us close to the heart of Christ. In the words of Saint John Paul II, they can become acts of "hollow ritualism." We might receive our first Communion and the sacraments of confession and confirmation, yet never experience the interior conversion that opens the heart to a personal relationship with God.

Pope Benedict XVI has explained that the "door of faith" is opened at one's baptism, but we are called to open it again, walk through it, and rediscover and renew our relationship with Christ and His Church.[38]

So how do we do this? How do we walk through that door of faith so we can begin to experience the abundant life that God has planned for us?

Getting Personal

The word *conversion* means "the act of turning." This means that conversion involves a turning away from one thing and a turning toward another. When you haven't experienced conversion of heart, you are turned *toward* your own desires. You are the one in charge, and you do what you feel is right and best at any given moment. You may choose to do things that are very good for other people, but the distinction is that *you are choosing*. You are deciding. You are the one in control.

Imagine driving a car. You are sitting in the driver's seat, and your hands are on the steering wheel. You've welcomed Jesus into the passenger's seat and have listened to His comments. But whether or not you follow His directions is really up to you. You may follow them or you may not, depending on what seems right to you.

When you experience interior conversion, you decide to turn, to get out of the driver's seat, move into the passenger's seat, and invite God to be the driver. Instead of seeing Him as an advice giver or someone nice to have around for the holidays, you give Him control of every aspect of your life.

More than likely, you don't find this easy to do. This is because of the universal struggle with pride. We want to be the ones in charge. We don't like to be in desperate need. We like to be the captains of our ships, charting our own courses. As William Ernest Henley wrote, "I am the master of my fate: I am the captain of my soul."

Conversion of heart isn't possible without humility. The first step is to recognize your desperate need of a savior. Romans 6:23 states that the "wages of sin is death." When you hear this, you might be tempted to justify your behavior, or compare yourself with others. You might think to yourself, "I'm not a murderer. I'm not as bad as this or that person. If someone were to put my good deeds and bad deeds on a scale, my good ones would outweigh the bad. So surely, I am good enough? Surely I don't deserve death!" When this is your line of thought, you are missing a very important truth: Just one sin is enough to separate you from a holy God. Just one sin is enough for you to deserve death. Even your best efforts to do good fall short of what God has required in order for you to spend eternity with Him. Isaiah 64:6 says, "All our righteous deeds are like a polluted garment." If you come to God thinking that you are going to be accepted by Him based on your "good conduct," He will point out that your righteousness is nothing compared to His infinite holiness.

Saint Thérèse of Lisieux understood this well, and wrote, "In the evening of my life I shall appear before You with empty hands, for I do not ask You to count my works. All our justices are stained in Your eyes. I want therefore to clothe myself in Your own justice and receive from Your love the eternal possession of Yourself."[39]

She recognized that her works, her best efforts, wouldn't be enough to earn salvation. Salvation cannot be earned. It's a free gift. Saint Thérèse accepted this gift and said that if her justices or righteous deeds were stained, then she wanted to clothe herself in Christ's own justice. We see this described in 2 Corinthians 5:21: "For our sake he made him to be sin who knew no sin, so that in him we might become the righteousness of God."

How did God make Him who had no sin to be sin for you? This was foretold by the prophet Isaiah: "But he was wounded for our transgressions, he was bruised for our iniquities; upon him was the chastisement that made us whole, and with his stripes we are healed." (Isaiah 53:5)

Jesus accomplished this on the cross. Every sin committed, past, present, and future, was placed on Him. Now, *all the merits of Jesus can be yours*. He wants to fill your empty hands with His own virtues.

But first, you need to recognize, just as Saint Thérèse did, that you are little. You are weak. You fail. You need forgiveness. You need a savior.

When you come before God in prayer and acknowledge these truths, He looks at your heart. He sees your desire to trust Him, to please Him, to obey Him. He says to you, "My precious child, you don't have to pay for your sins. My Son, Jesus, has already done that for you. He suffered, so that you wouldn't have to. I want to experience a relationship of intimacy with you. I forgive you.[40] Jesus came to set you free.[41] When you open your heart to me, you become a new creation![42] The old you has gone. The new you is here. If you will stay close to me, and journey by my side, you will begin to experience a transformation that brings joy and freedom.[43] I've been waiting to pour my gifts into your soul. Beloved daughter of Mine, remain confident in Me. I am your loving Father. Crawl into my lap. Trust me. Love me. I will take care of everything."

This is conversion of heart. This act of faith lifts the veil from your eyes and launches you into the richest and most satisfying life. You don't have to be sitting in church to do this. Don't let a minute pass before opening your heart to God and inviting Him to come dwell within you. Let Him sit in the driver's seat. Give Him the keys to your heart. Your life will never be the same again.

---

[40] "If we confess our sins, he is faithful and just, and will forgive our sins and cleanse us from all unrighteousness." 1 John 1:9.

[41] "So if the Son makes you free, you will be free indeed." John 8:36.

[42] "Therefore, if anyone is in Christ, he is a new creature; the old has passed away, behold, the new has come." 2 Corinthians 5:17.

[43] "I will sprinkle clean water upon you, and you shall be clean from all your uncleanness, and from all your idols I will cleanse you. A new heart I will give you, and a new spirit I will put within you; and I will take out of your flesh the heart of stone and give you a heart of flesh." Ezekiel 36:25, 26.

 NOTES

Appendix 3
CONCENTRIC CIRCLES OF FRIENDSHIP

On this page you will find circles that are labeled intimate friends, good friends, acquaintances, and social media relationships. Take a moment to fill in each circle with the names of the people in your life that fit the description best. Then take a look at who is in each circle. Are they where they should be? Is someone an intimate friend who should be a good friend? Is someone an acquaintance who you would like to become a good friend?

Writing these names out will help you to see and assess the intimacy of your relationship with their role in your life. Maybe you need to invest more deeply in one of your friendships or maybe toxic behavior requires that friendships become less intimate. The least number of names should be in your circle of intimate friendship. We are not capable of having more than a few deep, heart-level, intimate friends.

Note: You may be wondering why there is a place for social media relationships on the diagram. Oftentimes we count our relationships on social media as more intimate than they actually are. For a social media relationship to be significant, it needs to move from direct messaging to hanging out in person.

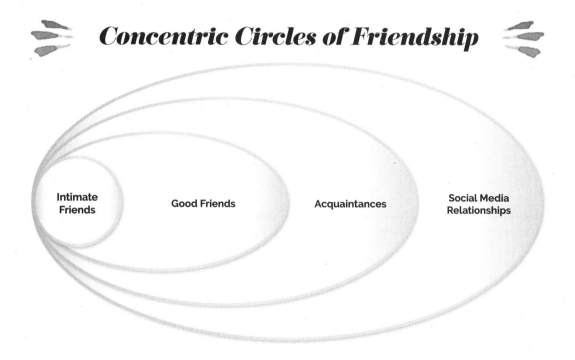

Concentric Circles of Friendship

Intimate Friends

Good Friends

Acquaintances

Social Media Relationships

NOTES

Answer Key

Lesson 2, Day One

1. God created the heavens and the earth in Genesis 1:1 and the Spirit of God was hovering over the waters in Genesis 1:2.
2. **A. John 1:1** The Word of God.
   B. The Word of God became flesh and dwelt among us. This is a description of the incarnation of Jesus. This incarnation is a teaching central to the Christian faith that God became a man by becoming Jesus. We believe that because of the incarnation, Jesus is fully God and fully man.
3. **A.** According to Acts 17:24-25, God does not need anything. We need Him for life and breath. He does not need us.
   B. CCC 1 God created us so that we can share in His own blessed life. We separated ourselves from Him by our sin, but God is constantly calling us back into His family. To accomplish this, He sent Jesus to redeem us and save us. We can now become His adopted children and heirs to His blessed life.
   C. CCC 221 We are destined to share in God's eternal exchange of love.
4. **A. CCC 27** Only in God will we find truth and happiness.
   B. To live fully according to the truth, we must accept that love and entrust ourselves to our creator.
5. Answers will vary.

Lesson 2, Day Two

1. **A.** "It is not good for man to be alone; I will make a suitable helper for him." (Genesis 2:18)
   B. Genesis 2:21–23 God places Adam into a deep sleep and created Eve from his rib, another person. Adam responds, "Finally, bone of my bone and flesh of my flesh."
2. **A. CCC 1878** Love of neighbor is inseparable from the love of God.
   B. CCC 1879 The human person needs to live in society. Through the exchange with others, mutual service and dialogue, man reaches his full potential.
3. **Genesis 3:12–14** Adam responded that Eve gave him the fruit, so he ate it. Eve responded that it was the serpent's deception that made her eat the apple.
4. Answers will vary.
5. **A. John 3:16–18** Our hope is in Jesus who came so that all who believe in Him will have eternal life. God sent Jesus, not to condemn the world but that it might be saved through Him.
   B. John 13:1–12 Jesus washes his disciple's feet in humble service.
   C. John 13:34–35 Jesus tells his disciples to love one another as He has loved them.

Lesson 2, Day Three

1. **A.** Sturdy shelter, treasure, priceless, life-saving medicine
    B. Those who fear the Lord.
2. **A.** We should be kind to others in our speech and in our manner. Our tongue should be gracious and courteous. We should seek to be at peace with people.
    B. Answers will vary; the second half of verse 6 advises to have one in a thousand.
    C. Because some people are only friends when it suits them but run away in times of trouble.
3. **John 15:13** Greater love has no one than this: to lay down one's life for one's friends.
4. Saint Paul said that he did not only want to share the Gospel with them, but he wanted to share his very life with them. This is an example of a virtuous friendship.
5. Answers will vary.
6. Answers will vary.

Lesson 2, Day Four

1. Jesus is telling the apostles (and us) to live in Him as He lives in them. He tells them that they can do nothing unless they remain in Him and says that those who don't remain in Him will be like branches that are thrown out. Those who remain in Him will bear much fruit. He says He has loved them as the Father has loved them and again tells them to remain in His love.
2. **A.** He said to abide in Him. To abide in Jesus means to stay in relationship with Him.
    B. He said that they need to keep His commandments.
    C. Jesus said that our joy would be in them and that their joy would be full.
    D. He commands them to love each other as I have loved you.
3. **A.** Two are better than one because they have a good return for their labor: It says that if one falls down, one can help the other up.
    B. They sharpen each other as iron sharpens iron.
    C. They had glad and generous hearts because they spent much time together in the temple and they broke bread at home.
4. Answers will vary.

Lesson 2, Day Five

1. Be completely humble and gentle; be patient, bearing with one another in love.
2. **A.** Romans 12:9-13 tells us to love each other by honoring one another above ourselves.
    B. Philippians 2:3 exhorts us to count each other more significant than yourselves.
3. Answers will vary.

4. Jesus was preaching in Capernaum, the crowd was so vast that there was no way to get to Jesus from the outside. Four men were carrying their friend on a stretcher. Unable to get to Jesus, they opened the roof and lowered him down. Jesus, because of their faith, healed the paralytic.

5. Answers will vary.

Lesson 3, Day One

1. **Psalm 103:15–16** A man's days are like grass; he flourishes like a flower of the field; for the wind passes over it, and it is gone, and its place knows it no more.
   Psalm 90:5–6 They are like a dream, like which is renewed in the morning and fades away in the evening.
   Psalm 144:3–5 They are like a breath. Their days are like a fleeting shadow.
   Psalm 39:5 Man's days are handbreadths, their lifetime is nothing in God's sight. Man is a breath.

2. We may gain a heart of wisdom.

3. He reveals himself to Peter, James, and John.

4. Answers will vary.

5. For everything there is a season, a time for every matter under heaven.

6. **A.** Answers will vary.
   B. Answers will vary.

Lesson 3, Day Two

1. He was betrayed by his equal companion, his familiar friend. They used to hold sweet converse together; within God's house they walked in fellowship.

2. Answers will vary.

3. He says to love your enemies and pray for those who persecute you, so that you may be sons of your Father who is in heaven.

4. David calls upon God.

Lesson 3, Day Three

1. **A.** They threw their cloaks down so Jesus could sit on the colt and they spread their cloaks on the road to honor him.
   B. The disciples sang praise to Jesus as they said, "Blessed is the King who comes in the name of the Lord! Peace in heaven and glory in the highest!"

2. Judas told the crowd that He would kiss the one to be arrested. Judas walked up to Jesus and kissed Him. The men then seized Jesus and arrested Him. Once Jesus was arrested, verse 50 says that they all forsook Him and fled.

3. Jesus tells Peter that he cannot follow Him now but can follow Him later. Peter asks why and says he would lay his life down for Jesus. Jesus responds by telling Peter that he will deny Him.
4. Answers will vary.
5. We are to speak truth in love and to grow up in every way into Him who is the head, into Christ.
6. **A.** Answers will vary.
   B. Answers will vary.

Lesson 3, Day Four

1. **A.** He compares the tongue to a bit that leads a horse, or a rudder that steers a ship. He makes this comparison because oftentimes, our tongues determine our direction.
   B. With the tongue we praise our God and curse human beings, who have been made in God's likeness. Saint James tells us that this should not be so.
2. **A.** The tongue has power over live and death.
   B. A man's religion is in vain if he does not bridle his tongue.
   C. A fool utters slander.
   D. A whisperer separates close friends because what she whispers is usually gossip. The things she is willing to say out loud directly to the person are rarely the problem. It's the things she wants to whisper that are often the most damaging. It's been said that "gossip is saying behind her back what you would not say to her face, and flattery is saying to her face what you would not say behind her back." Either way, it is not honest. We don't want to be caught in a lie. Is that perhaps why we whisper?
   E. They are compared to delicious morsels that go into the inner parts of the body. This means that there is a reason we enjoy gossip. Finding out other people's business is entertaining, intriguing and we don't normally forget it. The words of a whisper stick with us and affect how we see the person who is the subject of the gossip.
   F. Answers will vary.
3. Answers will vary.
4. Luke 6:45 says, "Out of the abundance of the mouth the heart speaks." The state of our hearts determines how we speak.
5. Answers will vary.
6. We should be quick to listen, slow to speak and slow to anger.

Lesson 3, Day Five

1. **A.** It rots the bones.
   B. You find disorder and every evil practice where you find envy.
2. Answers will vary.
3. **A.** When the older brother found out what happened he became angry and refused to join the party. When his father asked him to join, he responded, "Listen! For all these years I have been working like a slave for you, and I have never disobeyed your command; yet you have never given me even a young goat so that I might celebrate with my friends. But when this son of yours came back, who has devoured your property with prostitutes, you killed the fatted calf for him!"
   B. He said to him, "Son, you are always with me, and all that is mine is yours. But we had to celebrate and rejoice, because this brother of yours was dead and has come to life; he was lost and has been found."
   C. Answers will vary.
4. No one can boast because we have been saved by grace through faith. This is not from ourselves, but a gift from God. We were created in Christ Jesus to do the good works that God prepared for us.
5. When we are baptized into Christ we clothe ourselves with Christ and are one in Christ. When we belong to Christ we become heirs of His promise.
6. **A.** Answers will vary.
   B. Answers will vary.

Lesson 4, Day One

1. **A.** Man did not glorify or give thanks to God and so his heart was darkened and he became foolish.
   B. They exchanged the truth of God for a lie and worshiped created things instead of the Creator.
2. It wounded man's nature and injured human solidarity.
3. Answers will vary.
4. **A.** Jesus told the apostles that His soul was sorrowful unto death.
   B. He turned to God the Father. He fell on His face and asked Him to take the cup away from Him. A second time, He told the Lord that He would do His will.
   C. No, He found the disciples sleeping both times that He checked on them. They were unable to stay up and pray.

5. Answers will vary.

   In prayer, you can pray God's word back to Him and it can help to change your perspective. A few good Bible verses to pray with when you are feeling lonely are: Psalm 139:7-10, Isaiah 41:10, Psalm 46:1, and Isaiah 54:10.

Lesson 4, Day Two

1. **A.** In verse 4, the people say, "Come, let us build ourselves a city, and a tower with its top in the heavens, and let us make a name for ourselves, lest we be scattered abroad upon the face of the whole earth."

   B. The Lord said, "And I will make of you a great nation, and I will bless you, and make your name great, so that you will be a blessing."

   C. In Genesis 11:4, man decides he will make a name for himself. In Genesis 12:2, God says He will make Abram's name great. The first is for the sake of man, the second is for the sake of God.

2. Answers will vary.

3. **A.** **Romans 12:3** says we should not think of ourselves more highly or lowly than we ought to, but we should think of ourselves with sober judgment according to what God has given us.

   B. It tells us to consider others as more significant than ourselves.

4. We should have unity of spirit, sympathy, love of others, a tender heart, and a humble mind. Do not return evil for evil, but bless others. We should keep our tongue from evil, do right, and seek and pursue peace.

5. We should seek to live peaceably with all as far as it depends on us. This is not always possible.

6. Answers will vary.

Lesson 4, Day Three

1. **A.** **Proverbs 22:24–25** Do not make friends with an angry person, you will learn from him and possibly get yourself into trouble.

   B. **Proverbs 13:20** When we associate with the wise, we become wise. When we associate with fools, we suffer harm.

   C. **Proverbs 14:7** Stay away from a fool, for you will not find knowledge on their lips.

   D. **1 Corinthians 15:33** Bad company corrupts good morals.

2. **A.** These verses tell us that we should live quietly and mind our own affairs. We should work with our hands and walk properly before outsiders.

   B. We are responsible for our own work and decisions. When we stand before God, we will be standing alone. Ultimately, our total dependence should be on Him.

C. Be subject to one another out of reverence for Christ. When both parties regard the other as more important than themselves, the needs of both individuals are met.

D. We are supposed to use our speech for building others up, as it fits the occasion. We are to speak in such a way that we bestow grace on all who hear us.

3. Answers will vary.

4. A. In Matthew 18, Jesus directs us, "If your brother sins against you, go and tell him his fault, between you and him alone. If he listens to you, you have gained your brother. But if he does not listen, take one or two others along with you, that every word may be confirmed by the evidence of two or three witnesses. If he refuses to listen to them, tell it to the Church; and if he refuses to listen even to the Church," then it is ok to end the relationship.

B. In his Letter to Titus, Saint Paul says that we should avoid foolish controversies because they are unprofitable and worthless. As for a person who stirs up division, we should approach them.

5. Answers will vary.

Lesson 4, Day Four

1. A. **2 Corinthians 5:17** Anyone in Christ is a new creation. The old has passed and the new has come.

B. **Proverbs 4:23** Keep your heart with all vigilance because from our heart flows the spring of life.

C. **Colossians 3:1–2** He commands us to seek the things that are above. We should set our minds on things that are above, not on things that are on earth.

2. Answers will vary.

3. A. **Matthew 5:37** He said that our yes should mean yes, and our no should mean no, anything more is from the evil one.

B. No, Jesus often left the crowds to go and pray. In Mark 6:46, He left His disciples to pray, and Luke 6:12 says that He would spend all night with God.

C. No, He didn't. In Mark 6, Jesus did no mighty deed in Nazareth because of their lack of faith.

4. Answers will vary.

Lesson 4, Day Five

1. A. He owed him ten thousand talents and was unable to pay it back.

B. He asked him to be patient with him, and he would repay the debt.

C. He showed his servant compassion and forgave him the loan.

2. **Psalm 103:10–12** says that God does not deal with us according to our sins. His love is steadfast, and He casts our sin as far as the east is from the west.
   Romans 6:23 says that the wage of sin is death. The payment we owe for our sin is death, but God in His goodness offers us the gift of eternal life in Christ Jesus.
   Psalm 130:3–4 says that no one could stand if God marked our iniquities but with Him there is forgiveness.
3. Answers will vary.
4. Answers will vary.
5. The same servant came upon a fellow servant who owed him a hundred denarii. He seized him by the throat and demanded that the debt be paid. His fellow servant asked for mercy, but he threw him in jail. When the master found out, he threw him in jail saying, "You wicked servant, I forgave you all the debt because you besought me, shouldn't you have had mercy on your fellow servant?"
6. Answers will vary.

Lesson 5, Day One

1. **A.** The woman in this passage has been hemorrhaging blood for twelve years; she has sought healing at the hand of many doctors and spent all that she had trying to do it. It did not work.
    B. She had heard about Jesus and thought that if she could only touch His cloak, she would be made well. That's what she did and immediately the flow of blood stopped, and she felt in her body that she was healed of her disease.
    C. He told her that her faith had saved her; He then commanded her to go in peace and be healed.
2. God in His great love for us brought us to life even though we were dead in our sins. He raised us up with Him to sit with Him in the heavenly places in Christ Jesus. He saved us through His grace and created us in Christ for good works.
3. Answers will vary.
4. We respond by setting our hearts on things above, not on earthly things and by walking by the Spirit, not gratifying the desires of our flesh.
5. **A.** The sins described by Saint Paul are immorality, impurity, licentiousness, idolatry, sorcery, enmity, strife, jealousy, anger, selfishness, dissension, party spirit, envy, drunkenness, and carousing.
    B. The fruits of the spirit are love, joy, peace, patience, kindness, goodness, gentleness and self-control.
    C. We are to live and walk by the Spirit.
6. Answers will vary.

Lesson 5, Day Two

1. Wisdom is better than silver or gold, more precious than jewels, better than everything we desire; she brings with her a long life, riches, and honor. The ways of wisdom are pleasant. Wisdom leads to peace. She is like a tree of life and those who hold fast to wisdom are happy.

2. **Proverbs 13:16** Wise people think before they act; fools don't. Fools brag about their foolishness.

   Proverbs 12:15 The way of fools seems right to them, but the wise listen to advice.

   Proverbs 10:14 The wise lay-up knowledge, but the babbling of a fool brings ruin near.

3. Answers will vary.

4. **A.** Psalm 111:10 says that fear of the Lord is the beginning of wisdom.

   B. Proverbs 3:5 tell us to trust in the Lord with all your heart, and do not lean on your own understanding.

   C. James 1:5 tells us that if we are lacking wisdom, we should ask for it.

5. In Colossians 2:2–3 we learn it is Christ in whom are hidden the treasures of wisdom and knowledge.

6. Answers will vary.

Lesson 5, Day Three

1. **A.** According to Philippians 1:27, we are to let our manner of life be worthy of the Gospel of Christ. We are to stand firm in one spirit, with one mind striving for the faith of the Gospel.

   B. We are to be holy in all our conduct.

   C. "For if anyone is a hearer of the word and not a doer, he is like a man who observes his natural face in a mirror; for he observes himself and goes away and at once forgets what he was like. But he who looks into the perfect law, the law of liberty, and perseveres, being no hearer that forgets but a doer that acts, he shall be blessed in his doing."

   D. The definition of virtue according to the Catechism is, "a habitual and firm disposition to do good. It allows the person not only to perform good acts, but to give the best of himself. The virtuous person tends toward the good with all his sensory and spiritual powers; he pursues the good and chooses it in concrete actions. The goal of a virtuous life is to become like God."

2. Answers will vary.

3. **Prudence** is the ability to discern our true good in every circumstance and choose the right way to achieve that good.

Justice is the constant and firm will to give their due to God and neighbor. Giving God His due means to give Him worship. To give one's neighbor his due is to act fairly, impartially, and uprightly towards others.

Fortitude is firmness in difficulties and constancy in the pursuit of the good. It strengthens the resolve to resist temptations and to overcome obstacles in the moral life. The virtue of fortitude enables one to conquer fear, even fear of death, and to face trials and persecutions.

Temperance is self-control that moderates our attraction to pleasures and helps us to balance our use of created goods. It ensures the will's mastery over our instincts and keeps our desires within the limits of what is honorable.

4. **A.** Saint Paul explains that the law is spiritual but that he is in the flesh. He does not understand his own actions. He does what he doesn't want to do, the very thing he hates.

    B. The virtuous life is not easy because we are wounded by sin, so it is difficult for us to maintain a moral balance. God's grace, however, enters in and helps us to achieve these virtues. Virtues are acquired by education, deliberate acts, and perseverance ever-renewed in repeated efforts are purified and elevated by divine grace. He uses virtues to forge our character, and He helps us to be happy in practicing a virtuous life. We can respond to the grace God offers us by frequenting the sacraments, cooperating with the Holy Spirit, and following His call to love what is good and shun evil.

5. Answers will vary.

Lesson 5, Day Four

1. **A. Exodus 21:23–2** If a wrong is committed, this is the consequence that should follow: life for life, an eye for an eye, a tooth for a tooth, a hand for a hand, a foot for a food, burn for burn, wound for wound, strip for stripe.

    B. If a man causes a disfigurement in his neighbor, it shall be done to him as he did: "fracture for facture, eye for eye, tooth for tooth" (Leviticus 24:20).

    C. This approach was based on what is fair.

2. Jesus said that instead of following "an eye for an eye" and treating others how they have treated us, we go the extra mile. If someone strikes our cheek, we should offer them the other one, always going further than is commanded or asked of us.

3. Answers will vary.

4. Jesus meets a woman at a well in Samaria. She is drawing water in the middle of the day, and Jesus asks her for a drink. She is surprised because He is a Jewish man who is speaking to a Samaritan woman. Jesus speaks to her about living water

which is a bit confusing to the woman. He then tells her to call her husband, and she tells Him that she doesn't have a husband. He tells her that she has had five husbands and that the one she has now isn't her husband. The woman perceives that Jesus is a prophet. They begin to talk about worship of God, and Jesus reveals to her that He is the Messiah. At the end of the exchange, the woman leaves her jar and runs to the town people, the very people whom she was trying to avoid by drawing water in the middle of the day, and tells them that she met Jesus, who told her everything she had ever done. Because of her testimony, many Samaritans in that town came to believe in Jesus. Through the exchange, Jesus is kind. He does not judge or condemn her, but His love for her is grounded in Truth.

5. Answers will vary.

Lesson 5, Day Five

1. **A.** Jesus said to the Pharisee, "Do you see this woman? I entered your house, you gave me no water for my feet, but she has wet my feet with her tears and wiped them with her hair. You gave me no kiss, but…she has not ceased to kiss my feet. You did not anoint my head with oils, but she has anointed my feet…her sins, which are many, are forgiven, for she loved much."

    B. Answers will vary.
    - She did not wait for Jesus to acknowledge her but with tenacity initiated the act of love toward Him.
    - She showed Jesus extravagance in her actions not holding back but anointing Him with expensive oil.
    - She was not worried about rejection or public opinion; she actually made a fool of herself in her bold act of love.

2. Answers will vary.
3. He tells us that there is no fear in love and that perfect love drives out fear.
4. Jesus tells us to give, and it will be given to you. And that the measure with which we love will be measured back to us.
5. Answer will vary.

Prayer Pages

Opening

walking with purpose

A Prayer For Reclaiming Friendship: God's Plan for Deep Connection

Heavenly Father,

You have created me out of Your goodness and love
for a relationship with You and others.

Thank You for the beautiful gift of friendship and for every person
I have ever called a friend.

Thank You for the women who have been a sturdy shelter
and a life-saving medicine in my life—for the women
who have challenged me to become better,
have comforted me in sorrow,
and laughed with me through the joys of life.

Please heal me from friendships gone wrong
and bring comfort to those I have hurt.

Lord, move in me so that I may become the kind of friend
who is a gift to others—who loves at all times.

Lord, become the center of my friendships
so that we would bring glory to You
and reveal Your faithfulness to the world.

Amen.

Prayer Requests

Date:

Date:

Prayer Requests

Date:

Date:

Prayer Requests

Date:

Date:

 NOTES

Journal Your Prayers & Grow Closer to God

The Walking with Purpose *Praying from the Heart: Guided Journal* is a beautiful, comprehensive prayer journal that provides a private space to share your thoughts and feelings with the Lord.

Journaling your prayers lets you express a greater depth of intimacy toward God, and it will help you cultivate the practice of gratitude. Journaling will motivate you to pray regularly, too!

Praying from the Heart lays flat for easy writing, and is fashioned after the way that author Lisa Brenninkmeyer journals her own prayers. You'll love the heavyweight paper, luxurious leatherette cover, and many other special details.

shop.walkingwithpurpose.com

walking with purpose

SO MUCH MORE THAN A BIBLE STUDY

Walking with Purpose Devotionals

Daily affirmations of God's love

Rest: 31 Days of Peace

- A beautiful, hardcover, pocket-sized devotional to take wherever you go.

- 31 Scripture-based meditations that you can read (and re-read) daily.

- Become saturated with the truth that you are seen, known, and loved by a God who gave everything for you!

Be Still: A Daily Devotional to Quiet Your Heart

- Grow closer to the Lord each day of the year with our 365-day devotional.

- This beautifully designed hardcover devotional collection will renew your mind and help you look at things from God's perspective.

- Apply what you read in *Be Still*, and you'll make significant progress in your spiritual life!

shop.walkingwithpurpose.com

walking with purpose

~ SO MUCH MORE THAN A BIBLE STUDY ~

"For to the one who has, more will be given"
Matthew 13:12

The Journey Doesn't End Here

~ Christ's Love Is Endless ~

Walking with Purpose is more than a Bible study, it's a supportive community of women seeking lasting transformation of the heart. And you are invited.

Walking with Purpose believes that change happens in the hearts of women – and, by extension, in their families and beyond – through Bible study and community. We welcome all women, irrespective of faith background, age, or marital status.

Connect with us online for regular inspiration and to join the conversation. There you'll find insightful blog posts, videos, and free scripture printables.

For a daily dose of spiritual nourishment, join our community on Facebook, Twitter, Pinterest and Instagram.

And if you're so moved to start a Walking with Purpose study group at home or in your parish, take a look at our website for more information.

walkingwithpurpose.com

walking with purpose

~ SO MUCH MORE THAN A BIBLE STUDY ~

Transformative Catholic Bible Studies

Walking with Purpose Bible studies are created to help women deepen their personal relationship with Christ. Each study includes many lessons that explore core themes and challenges of modern life through the ancient wisdom of the Bible and the Catholic Church.

Opening Your Heart

A thoughtful consideration of the fundamental questions of faith – from why and how to pray to the role of the Holy Spirit in our lives and the purpose of suffering.

Living In the Father's Love

Gain a deeper understanding of how God's unconditional love transforms your relationship with others, with yourself, and most dearly, with Him.

Keeping In Balance

Discover how the wisdom of the Old and New Testaments can help you live a blessed lifestyle of calm, health, and holiness.

Touching the Divine

These thoughtful lessons draw you closer to Jesus and deepen your faith, trust, and understanding of what it means to be God's beloved daughter.

Discovering Our Dignity

Modern-day insight directly from women of the Bible presented as a tender, honest, and loving conversation–woman to woman.

Beholding His Glory

Old Testament Scripture leads us directly to our Redeemer, Jesus Christ. Page after page, God's awe-inspiring majesty is a treasure to behold.

Beholding Your King

This study of King David and several Old Testament prophets offers a fresh perspective of how all Scripture points to the glorious coming of Christ.

Grounded In Hope

Anchor yourself in the truth found in the New Testament book of Hebrews, and gain practical insight to help you run your race with perseverance.

Fearless and Free

With an emphasis on healing and wholeness, this study provides a firm foundation to stand on, no matter what life throws our way.

Choose your next Bible study at
shop.walkingwithpurpose.com

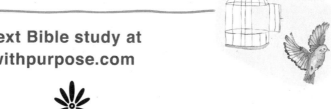

walking with purpose
SO MUCH MORE THAN A BIBLE STUDY

Share your faith with the next generation

Discovering My Purpose is a six-session Bible study designed for girls in their tween/teen years. This Bible study opens girls' eyes to their unique purpose, gifts, and God's love. It includes the BLAZE Spiritual Gifts Inventory, a fabulous tool to help girls discern where God is calling them to be world-changers.

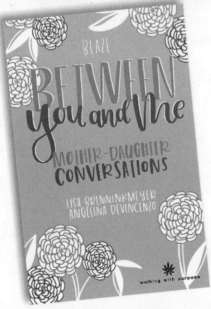

Between You and Me is a 40-day conversation guide for mothers and daughters to read together. Each day compares a lie of our secular culture with the truth found in Scripture. The daily reflection, discussion questions, and prayer prompts will springboard the mother/daughter relationship to a new level of honesty and intimacy.

BLAZE Masterpiece **BLAZE Belong**

- 20-lesson programs designed to help you lead any size group of middle school girls to a closer relationship with Christ.

- Both programs include BLAZE Kits, which are full of fun materials and take-home gifts that correspond with each lesson.

- BLAZE gives you the tools to speak to girls about their true identity as beloved daughters of God!

Learn more at walkingwithpurpose.com/blaze

walking with purpose
~ SO MUCH MORE THAN A BIBLE STUDY ~

Deepen Your Relationship with Christ

Catholic Bible Studies for Young Women

- Meeting young women where they are and pointing them to a life of freedom in Christ

- Based on our popular Bible studies for adult women and written especially for women in their late teens and twenties

- Each study guide contains five or six lessons to help apply Scripture to your daily life

- Great for personal meditation and group discussion

- Sold separately and in three-book sets: shop.walkingwithpurpose.com

Find great resources and tools to strengthen your Bible study experience!

walkingwithpurpose.com/young-adults

walking with purpose

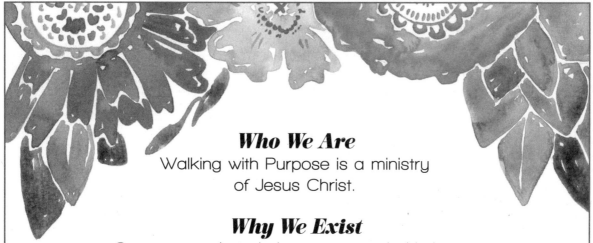

Who We Are
Walking with Purpose is a ministry
of Jesus Christ.

Why We Exist
Our purpose is to help women and girls know
Jesus Christ personally by making Scripture and the
teachings of the Catholic Church relevant and applicable.

Our Mission
Our mission is to help every Catholic woman and girl in
America encounter Jesus Christ through our Bible studies.

Our Vision
Our vision for the future is that, as more Catholic
women deepen their relationships with Jesus Christ,
eternity-changing transformation will take place in their
hearts – and, by extension – in their families, in their
communities, and ultimately, in our nation.

walking with purpose
⌒ SO MUCH MORE THAN A BIBLE STUDY ⌒

You can support our mission through a tax-deductible gift.
Learn more at walkingwithpurpose.com/donate